THE FIRST STATE BANK
and
(dis) TRUST
of Hinkley County

By: Craig Sullivan

Llumina
Press

© 2010 Craig Sullivan

All rights reserved. No part of this publication may be reproduced or transmitted in any form or by any means electronic or mechanical, including photocopy, recording, or any information storage and retrieval system, without permission in writing from both the copyright owner and the publisher.

Requests for permission to make copies of any part of this work should be mailed to Permissions Department, Llumina Press, 7915 W. McNab Rd., Tamarac, FL 33321

ISBN: 978-1-62550-308-4 PB
        978-1-60594-408-1 HC
        978-1-60594-409-8 Ebook

Printed in the United States of America by Llumina Press

Library of Congress Control Number: 2009909927

Caricatures by Cartoonist David Adams

David Adams is a self-taught cartoonist and print-maker. He draws the comic strip *The Bean Family* for insertion with the City of Lima, Ohio's utility bills to raise money for the City Parks Capital Improvement Fund. David has been a Cartoonist since the 5th grade; exhibits linoleum and wood relief prints and drawings in regional art shows; reviews movies for local media and serves on the Lima City Council.

Cover art by GRANT SULLIVAN

CONTENTS

Chapter 1	1
Chapter 2	9
Chapter 3	15
Chapter 4	19
Chapter 5	27
Chapter 6	41
Chapter 7	47
Chapter 8	53
Chapter 9	59
Chapter 10	65
Chapter 11	69
Chapter 12	75
Chapter 13	85
Chapter 14	91
Chapter 15	95
Chapter 16	101
Chapter 17	105
Chapter 18	111
Chapter 19	119
Chapter 20	121
Chapter 21	125
Chapter 22	133
Chapter 23	139
Chapter 24	143
Chapter 25	145
Chapter 26	153
Chapter 27	157
Chapter 28	163
Chapter 29	169
Chapter 30	173
Chapter 31	179
Chapter 32	189
Chapter 33	201
Epilogue	209

Part I

Cast Of Characters

Chapter 1

The First State Bank and Trust Company of Hinkley County was established as a matter of revenge. Sinclair Roberts applied for a loan from the Hinkley Savings Bank to enlarge his dry goods store and open a second location in Cougar Falls. An esteemed board member of the Hinkley Savings Bank, Reginald Van Pelt, happened to also own and operate a dry goods store in Cougar Falls and planned to expand his operation in Hinkley. He challenged the loan application on the grounds that Sinclair Roberts was known to associate with whores and reprobates of the lowest order—in addition to being Catholic.

The loan was denied.

Sinclair Roberts gathered three partners and, with four thousand dollars capital, founded the First State Bank and Trust Company of Hinkley County, and as the first order of business, he loaned himself three thousand dollars to expand his dry goods empire.

The bank prospered. Sinclair Roberts sold his dry goods business to Reginald Van Pelt and took up banking as a full-time vocation, eventually gaining fifty-one percent of the voting stock. Sinclair, at age sixty, assumed the position of chairman of the board and installed his eldest son Maurice Roberts as president of the bank.

Maurice studied law at the University of Notre Dame and had become comfortable in his position as teaching fellow and known carouser, associating with whores and reprobates of the lowest order while having a sexual preference that did not include women. Threatened with termination of his family's monthly contribution to his social education, he reluctantly returned to Hinkley to assume diluted leadership of the banking enterprise.

FIRST STATE BANK and (dis)TRUST of Hinkley County

Upon the death of Sinclair Roberts, Maurice took the opportunity to resign his position, take his sizable inheritance, and move to San Francisco where he opened a hair salon, indulging his hidden passion.

The bank fell upon hard times and had to recapitalize twice, reducing the family ownership to less than twenty percent.

Jerome Roberts, great-grandson of Sinclair by his youngest son Benedict, assumed control of the bank after marrying into a family descended from one of the founding partners and once again established controlling interest. Under his leadership, the bank prospered, celebrating a milestone of fifty million dollars of deposits and a plan to expand beyond the confines of Hinkley County into the uncharted, competitive market of Cougar Falls.

Jerome Roberts, known as J.R. to his friends and family, ran a tight ship, rarely delegating management responsibilities and tightly controlling privileged information. The bank's board of directors, comprised of his local parish priest, three business associates who rounded out his golfing foursome at the Hinkley Country Club, Hinkley County commissioner Ralph Bellows, a retired meat cutter, and the Hinkley High School principal Jerry Smithy, were all happy with their roles as silent directors, allowing J.R. to run the bank with no interference as long as the board meetings were followed by dinner and cigars at the country club along with an expense check.

J.R. arrived at the bank at eight-forty-five every morning, fifteen minutes before opening to the public, and he expected every employee to be at his or her respective post and working. He walked through the bank without acknowledging anyone, unlocked his office door, and hung his coat on the same wooden coat rack that Sinclair Roberts had used over one hundred years before and waited for his morning coffee and the *Wall Street Journal* to be delivered by his personal assistant.

"Good morning, Mr. Roberts," Sally Butterbetter said as she carefully set a large mug of coffee down on the desk along with his *Wall Street Journal* and the twice-weekly *Hinkley Messenger*. J.R. had hand-selected Sally from the

Hinkley High School graduating class five years prior after watching her progress and mature and receive her secretarial skills certificate.

Sally kept her hair lightly blond to accentuate her unusual emerald eyes and cut it shoulder-length with a seductive part falling ever so slightly over her impish face. She carried her petite frame with the grace of a ballet dancer, straight and statuesque, and always wore tight fitting business attire that accentuated the positives (and by everyone's estimation, vastly exceeded her financial means), was attentive to direction and mild reprimand, could not type or spell, but learned quickly how to screen calls and attend to the basic needs of a bank president.

"Good morning, Sally. How is Pastor Butterbetter? I hope he is healing quickly. I understand he took quite a nasty fall at the parsonage this last weekend." J.R. opened the *Journal* to the business section, and before Sally could respond about her father, the minister of the Body of Christ on the Cross Baptist Church, he said, "Get me the printouts of the overnight treasuries and the final numbers on the deposits for yesterday. And call Birdie at the club and tell her I need the corner booth for lunch."

"Yes, sir," Sally said with the concise tone of a private saluting a general. She methodically moved around the massive cherry desk, dragging her fingers around and over the protruding, hand-carved lion-head corners until she stood next to J.R., the full length of her high-heeled legs and protruding push-up bra enhanced breasts visible as she draped her arm over the back of the richly upholstered leather chair. The aroma of her Passion Princess perfume wafted past J.R.'s sensitive nose.

"Mrs. Witton from the Olatagwa Girl Scout conference called and asked to meet with you. It's cookie time, and she wants to take your order. And a 'Johnny,'" she hesitated and looked through the window behind his chair, as if attempting to recall the conversation, "from Executive Cars in Cougar Falls, I think, called and said they would be delivering your new Mercedes today. He wanted to know if they should bring it here or to your house." Sally turned back, smiling, overwhelmed with a sense of accomplishment after correctly reciting the messages.

FIRST STATE BANK and (dis)TRUST of Hinkley County

J.R. set the opened paper down on the desk, turned his head, and gave Sally a stern look. "Sally, how many times have I told you I do not want personal deliveries made to this bank? This is a business, not a damn receiving center, and our customers don't need to see my new Mercedes. What if Fred Ribley pulled into the lot about the time they're showing me how to run the confounded thing?"

Fred Ribley owned the local Ford dealership and ran his floor plan through the bank.

"Sally, sometimes I wonder."

Her bottom lip started to quiver and tears welled in those big green eyes.

He held up his hands. "Okay, no harm done. Let's not get all emotional here; it's only nine o'clock, and we have a long day. Go get those reports, and and,maybe go take a break or something. And don't forget, we have a board meeting tonight. You didn't forget, did you?"

She wiped her right eye with her sleeve, smearing mascara across her cheek, and let a wry smile emerge. "No, I didn't forget."

At fifty-two, Jerome Roberts kept physically fit, with the exception of a few extra pounds that gathered around his belt. He still had thick black hair with just a hint of gray filtering through at the temple, and he had that colored on a regular basis. He wore only British tailored suits, hand fitted and imported by Austin and Jones, a Chicago haberdashery. His drink of choice was single malt scotch purchased by the case. His marriage was one of necessity rather than choice, the necessity being the acquisition of a sizable block of State Bank voting stock. The passion necessary to achieve his goal of securing the stock had long since been exhausted, so J.R. devoted his free time and considerable expendable income to collecting expensive cars, trucks, motor homes, boats, and vacation homes. His remaining passion, not wasted on his wife, was put to good use on those who were attracted to expensive cars, trucks, motor homes, boats, and vacation homes.

The third Tuesday of each month was board night; his board of directors gathered to review the bank's cash flow and any new items or large loan applications that required review, although that never happened because J.R. had the final say, so the meeting generally consisted of gossip about the personal lives of other members of the country club or other business associates in town.

Ralph Bellows, a county commissioner, was usually half in the bag by the time the meeting started, so his input, audible but sometimes not understandable, was useless. Father Tom came to enjoy the expansive and overpriced menu offered by the country club along with a couple of "toots," as he called them, to make him sleep. Jerry Smithy, the Hinkley High School principal, cherished the opportunity to hobnob with the elite businessmen of the community who lounged around the bar of the club and get a night away from his nagging wife.

The other board members, Sid Johnson, owner of Sid's Contracting; Jason Roberts, owner of Roberts's Funeral Home, Crematorium, and Florist, J.R.'s first cousin; and Fred Chin Lee, owner of Chin Lee's Dry Cleaning, were all golfing buddies of J.R. and couldn't care less about the operation of the bank as long as their small stock holdings were awarded quarterly dividends.

Prior to the meeting, J.R. had a private lunch at the country club, reviewed the agenda for the meeting, and prepared written minutes of how the meeting should flow and be conducted, following accepted rules of order and including all the detail federal bank examiners expected to see when they made their quarterly review at the bank. He had the minutes transcribed, typed, and copied before the meeting ever took place, understanding that the actual board meeting was little more than a bull session before dinner.

When he arrived at the club for his noon lunch, his booth was reserved and waiting. Jotting down motions and voting tabulations as if he were the recording secretary at an actual meeting, interspersed with an occasional bite of his blackened salmon salad, he didn't notice his wife Monica approach the booth. She had arrived to participate in her canasta club dressed

FIRST STATE BANK and (dis)TRUST of Hinkley County

in up-scale casual attire that draped her nearly two-hundred-pound girth like a tent. She had been advised to avoid horizontal stripes so she concentrated on loose-fitting jump suits that gave her the appearance of a work-out-bound sumo wrestler.

"Had I known you were going to lunch at the club, I could have joined you," she said sarcastically, "but we both know that invitation got lost in the mail."

J.R. looked up, inspected her attire, and said without much enthusiasm, "Decide to jog to the club today?"

Monica's face reddened and her nostrils flared, giving her the appearance of a ripe apple atop a whiskey barrel. She opened her mouth to respond but realized she was standing within earshot of other diners and club members, so turned and stomped out of the room.

Jim Wagner, a local insurance agent and self-proclaimed investment counselor sat at the bar consuming a gin martini for lunch. He saw Monica abruptly leave and casually sauntered over to J.R.'s booth, cradling his long-stemmed martini glass and looking toward the door. "Monica couldn't join you for lunch, huh?" He glanced at the papers spread across the table. "Busy day at the bank?"

"Board meeting tonight," J.R. responded, without looking up or extending an invitation for Wagner to join him.

Wagner scooted into the big booth anyway. "How's the bank doing these days, J.R.? You struggling like everyone else? I mean—all of this bailout stuff—huge banks failing left and right. I've never seen it this bad before."

J.R. had no choice but to entertain the question. It was either answer and continue the conversation or offend Wagner, which was not easy to do. "We're holding our own and still paying a dividend now and then. Careful with that martini; don't want gin all over my notes for tonight's meeting." The precaution was meant to suggest that Wagner go back to the bar.

Wagner picked up his glass, downed the remains with one gulp, looked across the room at the bartender, and held up the glass. "You guys getting any of the free money?" He chuckled. "If you do, spread some my way. The market's about dried up my portfolio."

"I thought you were the investment guru. How did you get caught with your pants down?" It was a test of Wagner's leather façade. How much insult could he take before he realized the waters were calmer back at the bar? "Things must be tough when you have to drink your lunch."

"It's not just me, man. You know that. It's the whole fucking system, from the top to the bottom. Everyone's getting screwed except the politicians and the big bank executives." The bartender brought Wagner's refill, and they exchanged glasses. "Present company excluded, of course."

"Well, we still pay one percent on passbook and two and a half on a two-year CD. How many of your clients earned two and a half percent on their investments last year with no loss in principle?"

"You don't have to get personal, J.R. I'm just making conversation, concerned about the state of our economy. Hell, both of our incomes are dependent on how this all shakes out. Seriously, what's the chance of getting a short-term loan? You know, 'til things get back to normal?" Wagner took a long draw on his martini, set the glass down, and with glassy eyes waited for J.R.'s response.

"Seriously, Jim?" J.R. said, using the same inquisitive tone; then after lingering silence said with deadpan sincerity, "None."

Wagner stared at J.R. and said, "Well, fuck you very much." He got up and staggered back to the bar.

J.R. Roberts

CHAPTER 2

The board meeting convened in a private room off the main dining room of the Hinkley Country Club. The solid walnut tandem doors with a hand-carved Hinkley Club crest embedded in the middle of each offered plenty of privacy for the meeting. Each member of the board arrived separately and lounged at the bar, or in the case of Father Tom, sat at the conference table eating the appetizers he had ordered from the menu. Ralph Bellows, not a member of the club, always took the opportunity on board night to sit at the bar all afternoon, padding J.R.'s tab. By the time the meeting started, if he lasted that long, which often he did not, he was only semi-conscious. Jerry Smithy arrived early and worked the room, shaking hands with members, reminiscing about the high school, and generally enjoying his temporarily elevated status in the community. The remaining board members played a round of golf before the meeting during the season and during the off-season played gin in the locker room until the meeting convened.

FIRST STATE BANK and (dis)TRUST of Hinkley County

At seven o'clock, J.R. called the meeting to order. All members were present, with the exception of Ralph Bellows.

"Anyone seen Ralph?" J.R. asked, looking around the table.

"I saw him at the bar earlier," Father Tom said, "but he was having trouble deciding what he wanted to drink next, so I didn't want to interrupt."

J.R. picked up the house phone and called the bar. "Jimmy, Ralph Bellows still there? Uh-huh, uh-huh. Well, send someone down there and wake him up. He's supposed to be in here for our board meeting." He hung up the phone and shook his head. "We'll start without him. He's down in the locker room, passed out. It's beyond me how that drunken fool keeps getting elected. Okay, you all have the minutes of tonight's meeting in front of you. Have any questions?"

No one except Father Tom bothered to look at the papers, and he held the prepared minutes out at arm's length. "Let's see. We approve the minutes of the last meeting. Yes, I see they are here. Okay, we discuss the latest earnings and expense report given by the treasurer, Fred. Then we move to accept, yes, okay."

J.R. interrupted Father Tom. "Okay, if there are no further comments or questions, we can move on." His tone and glare were all that was necessary to make Father Tom slump back in his chair. "We are declaring a dollar and twenty-cent quarterly dividend, the same as the last three quarters. Things are tightening up, but we are still in the black."

The mention of a dividend check sparked Fred Chin Lee's interest, and he looked up from the golf scorecard he had been tallying and said, "When is that going to go up? We are spending a lot of money on this new location; maybe we could think about increasing the dividend." Fred owned five hundred shares of stock, a paltry sum compared to J.R.'s forty-two thousand shares. The bank had eighty thousand outstanding shares of voting stock.

"Fred, don't get greedy, okay? Do you realize ninety percent of the banks in this country have either cut dividends or eliminated them completely? First Fidelity cut their dividend in half this quarter. If they make it through the next six months, and there's a good chance they won't, I suspect there won't be any distribution at all next year. At least for now, big isn't better. So I would suggest that you and the rest of the stockholders be thankful we are still flush." J.R. pushed some papers around in front of him trying to contain his anger while Fred belched, giving the impression that the conversation was giving him heartburn, and went back to penciling arithmetic on his scorecard.

J.R. pulled a bundle of papers from his briefcase and after pulling off some rubber bands set the papers down and said, "The Federal Reserve has been sending this stuff on a daily basis, trying to explain how we got in this financial crisis, or whatever they are calling it this week."

Before J.R. could get to the meat of his topic, the doors swung open, and Ralph Bellows staggered in, carrying a drink in one hand and a towel in the other. He stopped and toweled some of the refreshment off the front of his shirt, looked up, smiled, and said, "Time for dinner?"

Ralph was short, mostly bald, had a bad case of rosacea—causing his nose to be a bulbous red blob in the middle of his face—and was drunk for most of his waking hours. If there were a standard description and brochure for a retired butcher, Ralph's picture would be on the cover. His only close encounter with the law was being arrested for riding his horse down Main Street on Saint Patrick's Day in a less than sober condition, so much less than sober that he broke his arm when he fell off the horse after being stopped by the highway patrol. The story played well on the front page of the *Hinkley Messenger,* but most of the county inhabitants knew Ralph and merely had a good laugh at his expense. Unfortunately, Red Redderson, the editor of the paper, saw the opportunity to get the *Messenger's* name distributed nationally and put the picture of Ralph on his horse standing next to the officer and patrol car on the *Associated Press* national wire service, sending it all over the country. The picture even ended up in David Letterman's *Late Night Show* monologue, giving Ralph his fifteen seconds of fame.

J.R. swung his chair around and gave Ralph the steely glare he usually reserved for his employees. "Nice that you could join us halfway through the meeting. Sorry we interrupted your nap." He turned back to the seated members and continued. "The feds are trying to get every bank to loosen up and lend money, no matter the need or who needs it. That's what got them into this mess to begin with, but in typical government fashion, logic is not a consideration."

Ralph made his way around the table, patting each member on the back as he guided his unstable mass toward a vacant chair. He pulled the chair out and inadvertently tipped his full glass of scotch, spraying the liquid across the table. "Cheese and crackers, that's ten-year-old scotch. Anyone want to lick the table?" Ralph said with a big guffaw.

"Ralph, damn it—sit down or go home. We're trying to conduct business here."

"But I haven't had dinner yet," Ralph whined as he toweled up the spillage.

J.R. sat back, crossed his arms with a disgusted sigh, and waited for Ralph to get settled. "If we can get back on the subject. The last communication I received—," he pawed through the mass of papers. "Here it is. Yusuf Hussein Olajuwon says he will be coming to the bank next week to—this is a good one. Listen to this. 'Set up our partnership agreement and discuss your T.A.R.P. participation.'"

Everyone at the table gave a hearty laugh, except Ralph, who had his hands clasped on his protruding girth, his eyes closed. He was starting to give faint, guttural snorts, a prelude to an all-out snore.

Jerry Smithy looked up from his menu and said, "I still can't figure out why they called it a tarp. It seems to me that 'blanket' would have been a better figure of speech." Jerry prided himself on his knowledge and use of the English language. "I mean, they are spreading money everywhere, as if they are blanketing the financial markets. They're not tarping it. That sounds like it burned or something." He glanced around the table, looking for acknowledgement of his intellectual acumen, but found none.

J.R. rubbed his face and replied, "Jerry, T.A.R.P. is an acronym for 'troubled asset relief program.' I don't think they could have come up with a program name that fit the letters in 'blanket.'"

Smithy sank back into his chair and held his menu close to his face.

J.R. continued, "First of all, I'm not going to partner with anyone from the government. Second, I'm not going to meet with any towel head named Yusuf Hussein. Sounds like some kind of terrorist or something."

"Be careful," Jason Roberts said as he perused the club menu. "The president's middle name is Hussein, you know. This could be his cousin or something. I'm sure he's got a whole flock of Husseins working in Washington by now."

Ralph's eyes popped open and he came to attention. "Terrorists? Where? Here? I'm a commissioner. Why didn't someone tell me about this? Do I need to call the sheriff?" His hand shook as he gulped down the last of his scotch. "Everyone just stay calm."

Everyone in the room looked at Ralph, dumbfounded.

"Shut up, Ralph, you moron," said J.R. "There are no terrorists. Nobody said anything about any terrorists. You've been dreaming."

"Moron? You call me a moron?" Ralph said, slurring his words badly. "I'm a county commissioner. I run this entire county," he said, swinging his arm, emphasizing his perceived importance. He pushed himself from the table. "I don't have to listen to this."

"Are you resigning your position as a board member of this bank, Ralph?" J.R. asked. "If you are, I'll have Sally bring the letter of resignation to your office tomorrow, first thing."

Ralph leaned on the table with his palms flat, trying to focus on the other members seated in front of him and thinking about the expense check he received each month after the meeting. "I, I,...... didn't say anything about resigning,......, did I?" He paused, licked his lips, and said, "I need a refill." He smiled and pushed himself back from the table. "Anyone else need anything? J.R.'s buying."

FIRST STATE BANK and (dis)TRUST of Hinkley County

J.R. concluded the meeting after Ralph left by saying he would deal with the Federal Reserve people in his own way and then excused himself from the gathering, saying he was going to dine alone and review other bank matters in private. He exited the private room, advised Miranda, the hostess, that the others were ready to order dinner, and walked past the bar without speaking to Ralph, who did not notice him anyway, and descended the stairs to the locker room. He called the bar and told Jimmy he was working in private and was not to be disturbed under any circumstances. From there, he exited the building from the back and made his way through the dark parking lot to his new Mercedes.

The Cougar Falls Best Western was a twenty-mile drive down the four-lane to the I-70 interchange. He hummed along with the Blaupunck-enhanced voice of Phil Collins as he drove, observing the speed limit, and smiling the entire distance. He parked well away from the building and any security cameras, walked to one of the rear exits, slid a key card through the slot and gained entrance as he had done several times before. He found room one-twenty-one and lightly knocked on the door.

He heard the security chain slide slowly off the guide and the dead bolt give way, and the door opened slightly.

"What's the password, big boy?" Sally said in a slow drawl, mimicking Mae West's sexy, low voice. "Why don't you come in? The party's just starting."

J.R. saw the lacy negligee through the crack in the door, one of three he had brought back from his last trip to Chicago and visit to Victoria's Secret. He slid through the door, replaced the safety chain, and left all thoughts of dividends, T.A.R.P. and Hussein in the Best Western hallway.

Ernest Eisley

CHAPTER 3

Ernest Eisley worked the State Bank drive-through window with the precision of a surgeon. He wore a rubber fingertip on his right thumb to help with his count. He always adjusted the paper currency face up to the left. His teller station was organized, his writing utensils placed in order—black pen, blue pen, red pen, and pencil. His plastic shirt-pocket writing utensil holder was managed in the same way.

He arrived at the bank by eight-twenty every morning, without fail the first to arrive and unlock the rear entrance. His bank always balanced on the first total at the end of the day, and with regard to his professional prowess as a bank teller, he had reached the very top of his class. He had even received the coveted Bank Teller of the Year award three years in a row, but due to unrest among the other tellers, he had been inducted into the State Bank's newly established Bank Tellers' Hall of Fame, giving one of the lesser-known tellers the opportunity to be recognized.

FIRST STATE BANK and (dis)TRUST of Hinkley County

Ernest carefully maintained his appearance; always wearing a white oxford shirt with neatly pressed black polyester pants. His pastel tie usually matched his socks. His wardrobe was prepared by his mother and hung in the hall closet every morning because she was not allowed entry into his locked bedroom.

He spent a full thirty minutes each morning in front of the bathroom mirror, carefully manipulating his closely cropped, thinning, pepper-brown hair with just a dab of Brill Cream to bring out the shine. His last touch was to place his black, horn-rimmed glasses on his face, step back, straighten his tie, smile, blow himself a kiss, and practice his bank teller greeting. "Good morning, Mrs. Myers. How may I help you?"

Ernest graduated from Hinkley High School with the same obscurity and mediocrity that he was now experiencing with his career at the bank. From high school, he enrolled in the Rawson Career Opportunity Center for Learning in Cougar Falls and studied nights for two years to receive his practical business principles certificate. Through the school's placement service and after an additional hefty fee, he was offered employment at the First State Bank and Trust Company.

From his first day on the job, Ernest showed great promise as a teller, diligently cleaning and polishing his fingernails each morning, realizing customers would concentrate on his fingers as he counted out their change. He brought his own lemon-scented spray disinfectant to keep his station clean and aromatically pleasing to his customers. He mentally catalogued each customer's name to assure a proper greeting. Ernest was, by everyone's definition, the perfect employee.

But Ernest had some personal baggage, qualities that were not mainstream for Hinkley, or, for that matter, anywhere.

At twenty-eight, Ernest lived with his mother in a small, two-bedroom house, just down the street from Hinkley High School.

From the first day Ernest was enrolled in the Hinkley school system, he was considered an unusual child. His mother picked him up with regularity mid-morning and mid-afternoon each day, and together they left in her antiquated station wagon, only to return fifteen minutes later, Ernest refreshed, with a rosy glint to his face. When queried about their excursions, Mrs. Eisley dismissed the issue, suggesting it was personal and beyond the scope of the school's authority.

Sometime during Ernest's third or fourth grade, Jerry Smithy, at that time the elementary school principal, was running a mid-morning errand in his big pickup truck, which gave him a good view of the inside of any vehicle next to him or stopped at an intersection. With considerable disbelief and shock, Principal Smithy saw in a vehicle next to him a pretty good-sized young man suckling on an older woman's breast.

When Mrs. Eisley's eyes met Principal Smithy's stare, there was no longer any question about what Ernest and his mother did on their daily excursions.

It was impossible to keep Principal Smithy's revelation from ramping through the Hinkley school system gossip mill. Within days, Ernest had the nickname "Pucker," a moniker that would follow him for the balance of his days in Hinkley.

Pucker, when not within the confines of his teller station, lived in a fantasy world that involved internet sexual encounters, bus trips to Cougar Falls to browse the adult book and video store, occasional ventures into cross-dressing—but only in his locked bedroom—and a fanatical obsession with Sally Butterbetter.

He sat in his teller station, which conveniently gave him a frontal view of Sally at her desk in front of Mr. Robert's office, and fantasized about their weekend motor trip. Of course, Sally would have to drive her fancy Japanese convertible because Pucker did not have a driver's license. He even envisioned Sally one day being his wife and sharing the pleasures of his locked bedroom, but only after his mother had retired and begun her rhythmic snore.

Unfortunately, Sally had not realized or fantasized about the quality relationship that awaited her with Pucker, at least not yet. Pucker was still in the initial stages of cultivating their potential future relationship. He had managed on occasion to

FIRST STATE BANK and **(dis)**TRUST of Hinkley County

walk past Sally while she sat at her desk and offer a morning greeting, which he religiously practiced in front of the mirror. "Isn't it just glorious outside today, Miss Butterbetter?"

So far, the best he had received in reply was, "Fuck off, Pucker."

Yusef Olajuwon

CHAPTER 4

By ten-fifteen, J.R. had perused the *Wall Street Journal*, downed his second cup of coffee, ordered a new GPS over the internet for his thirty-eight-foot cruiser moored at the city pier off Michigan Avenue in Chicago, and booked a room at the Bellagio in Las Vegas for the upcoming annual American Bankers' Association meeting. He was loading some personal papers into his briefcase in preparation to leave for the day and drive to Chicago to spend the weekend on his boat when Sally stepped through his office door. She had a disturbed look on her face and pushed the door closed behind her.

"J.R., there's a big black guy out here. I mean a *big* black guy," she said. She held a business card up to her face and read, "Yusuf Olajuwon," drawing out each syllable in an attempt to pronounce the name, "from the Department of the Treasury, Banking Division." She put the card down and covered her mouth with her hand to discourage a laugh. "Should I call the sheriff?"

FIRST STATE BANK and (dis)TRUST of Hinkley County

J.R. stared at the closed door, still holding the briefcase, and then looked up at Sally, who still stood with her hand over her mouth, wide-eyed in anticipation of his response.

"Tell him I don't meet with anyone without an appointment. If he wants to make an appointment, make it at least two weeks from now, but not on a Friday or a Monday." He went back to stuffing papers into the case and started to unplug his laptop and looked up to find Sally still standing in front of him with the same dysfunctional expression on her face. "Something wrong, Miss Butterbetter?"

"Uh, I guess not. But he says he's from the government. What if he don't want to leave? I mean, jeez, J.R., that's one big black guy."

"I know, you said that before. And don't use that poor English around here. You sound like you were born in a trailer."

As soon as he said it, he knew it was a mistake. Sally stuck her lower lip out and blinked twice, almost as if she was trying to produce a tear.

"Okay, I didn't mean that, but you need to... Well, you know, practice a little. Try not to—oh, just forget it. Go out and tell him what I said. He isn't going to do anything."

As the last word exited J.R.'s mouth, the office door swung open and Yusuf Olajuwon took a step into the doorway, encompassing the entire void in the wall. His silk suit shimmered from the sunlight filtering through the office window, and his closely cut hair had a reflective sheen that enhanced his amber skin and gave his deep, dark eyes a penetrating stare. He held out a hand with well-manicured nails and said in a baritone voice fit for a rendition of *Old Man River*. "Mr. Roberts, it's a pleasure to meet you. I'm Yusuf Olajuwon, midwest regional supervisor for the United States Department of Treasury, Banking Division."

J.R. sat, his mouth hanging open, staring at the man at first in awe, then with respect for his size, and then as the moment lingered and he regained his composure, disgust for the intrusion.

"Who do you think y-y-you are, busting in here w-w-without me saying y-you can bust in here?" J.R. had stuttered as a child and in intense situations, the vocal disability reinvented itself. "I-I-I don't care if y-y-you are the p-p-president of the United States; this is m-m-my bank and y-you cannot just w-w-walk in here."

Sally had never heard J.R. stutter, other than a few unintelligible repetitions during the heat of passion and stared at him, astonished, trying to hold back laughter. For some reason, the respect and fear she had previously held for J.R. incrementally disappeared with each stutter. Then she turned to Yusuf and said, "W-w-want to sit down?"

J.R. opened his mouth to protest, made eye contact with Sally and Yusuf, leaned back in his plush leather chair, sighed, and gave Sally a flitting hand signal indicating that she was dismissed.

Sally smiled at Yusuf, sashayed across the room, turned, and for the first time, at least as far as J.R. was concerned, gave him a smirk that seemed to suggest his position of respect had just dropped a few notches. The slam of the door confirmed the suspicion.

J.R. sat up, moved a couple of papers around on his desk, folded his hands, stared directly at Yusuf, and said without a stutter, "Okay, Mr. Big Government Official who waltzed in here without an appointment or an invitation, what can I do for you before I call the sheriff and have your black ass thrown out?"

Yusuf suppressed a chuckle and pursed his lips, suppressing the urge to laugh, and said, "Mr. Roberts, let's not allow our personal feelings about race, religion, and shall we say, patriotism, interfere with our common mission—saving our country from financial ruin. I realize this remote community is probably not used to the integration the rest of our country has adopted, but I assure you I am competent and well qualified to work with you and guide you and this bank to financial stability. I have a master's degree in finance from—"

J.R. interrupted, "I don't care if you are a Rhodes Scholar, and I wouldn't care if you were purple, red, Mexican, Chinese, or whatever. No one is going to walk into my bank and tell me how to run my business. Got that? *Capice?* Are we clear?"

FIRST STATE BANK and (dis)TRUST of Hinkley County

"I think you misunderstand the purpose of my visit, Mr. Roberts. I am not here to criticize your business practices or create any undue stress on you or your employees." Yusuf seemed to relax as he adjusted his suit jacket and ran his fingers down the pant crease of his crossed legs.

J.R. looked at his watch and then up at his visitor. "Well, I'm glad you made that clear. And now, if you will excuse me, I have an appointment with someone that was mannerly enough to arrange the meeting in advance. You want to see anything pertaining to the bank—financials or whatever—tell Sally, and she will direct you to the correct person, assuming our check of your credentials prove accurate." J.R. stood and picked up his briefcase. "Sorry you made the long drive from wherever you came from. Maybe next time you will call ahead." J.R. stood and waited behind his desk for Yusuf to make the next move in the cat and mouse game.

Yusuf did not change his demeanor, and if anything, sank deeper into the plush chair. "Once again, Mr. Roberts, I think you perhaps jumped to some unfair conclusions. We, the United States Treasury Department and I, are trying to stem the tide of a disastrous undercurrent of financial instability that could collapse our banking system. Do you understand?"

J.R. opened his mouth to respond, but Yusuf continued. "Now, the treasury secretary and Congress have made a large sum of capital available to both large and small banks, hoping to stimulate lending, interbank and consumer alike. There are certain—"

J.R. interrupted, holding up both hands as if he had surrendered. "Mister, uh, what is your name?"

"It's Yusuf, Yusuf Olajuwon."

"Okay, Mr. Yusuf Ola—whatever. Obviously, even with your educational credentials, you have some sort of listening disorder. Maybe I'm just not making myself clear. Please listen very carefully." He felt sweat gathering on his forehead and trickling down his recently colored hair onto his face. "I-I-I do not c-c-care w-w-what—" He stopped, took a deep breath, exhaled, closed his eyes, and concentrated on calming himself.

"I am trying to stay calm here, Mr. Yusuf. I am trying to be generous with my time and as polite as I can be without offending you, but you are making it very difficult." J.R. once again felt his face reddening and his blood pressure rising.

The door opened far enough for Sally to stick her head in and, after giving Yusuf a curious, almost flirtatious smile, turned grim and looked at J.R. "Need anything?"

"Sh-sh-shut the d-door now," J.R. roared, loudly enough to turn the heads of the customers in the teller lines. Lowering his head, he closed his eyes, drew a long breath, and tried to concentrate on a calming thought before looking up. He found Sally standing half in the doorway, displaying her lengthy legs and still smiling at Yusuf. He opened his mouth to bellow his command again, but Sally sensed his movement and withdrew with a ballerina-like spin on her toes.

J.R. cradled his forehead in his hand, his elbow propped on his desk.

Yusuf saw his opportunity. "Mr. Roberts, I can see you are a very busy man." With a slight hint of a smile, he looked at the closed door. "And you have a lot on your plate." He let the last assumption hang in the air. "I think it would be best if I just lay out our plan of action and your opportunity to participate in the rebuilding of America. I'm sure you know Illinois is the president's home state, so he takes particular interest in small rural communities like yours. His mandate is to start from the bottom and create a grass-roots revival of the banking industry. And as you know, banks control the economy, and as the banks go so goes the country's economic health."

Yusuf stopped. J.R., though staring at him, had a distant look in his eyes, almost as if he were looking beyond Yusuf at some distant object. He was tempted to turn and see if something or someone was behind him, drawing J.R.'s attention. "Uh, are you okay, Mr. Roberts? You seem distracted."

Yusuf was right. J.R. had wandered off to a place far away, thinking about his boat and the lapping waves lulling him to sleep; the string bikini-clad young girls walking the docks all day long; his iced scotch sitting on the rear deck of his yacht as the sun set broke the surface of Lake Michigan.

"Look, Mr. Yusuf, maybe we should do this another time, when I can—"

Yusuf interrupted. "The thing is, Mr. Roberts—J.R.—you don't mind if I call you J.R., do you?" He did not allow time for a reply. "We really don't have time to delay this conversation. See," Yusuf leaned forward in his chair, "right now, our economy sucks, and that's an understatement. The treasury department has made it clear that those of us in the field are to take dramatic steps to get things rolling again. Do you understand me, J.R.? That means me and you got to go to the dance, and we ain't got time to get dressed up."

Yusuf's change in vernacular caught J.R. off-guard and brought him back to reality. "I guess I don't follow your dance metaphor, Mr. Yusuf, because I don't plan on going anywhere with you."

"J.R., I don't think you understand." Yusuf stood and towered over J.R.'s desk. He ran his hand over the carved lion head protruding from the corner of the desk as if he were caressing a pet cat. "J.R., J.R., J.R.," he said in a condescending manner. "What would the people of this community think if they knew you refused to help our country in its time of need? You never served in the armed forces, so maybe they would understand that instead of doing the patriotic thing, you continued to muddle through life, spend time on your expensive yacht, and drive your expensive cars." He looked again at the closed door. "Not to mention other extracurricular activities I am sure you prefer not to discuss."

J.R. abruptly raised, both hands on his desk, and leaned close to Yusuf, who still towered over him, and said slowly, emphasizing each syllable, "Get your slick-suited black ass out of my office."

"Calm down; I didn't mean to get personal. I just wanted to let you know that we do our due diligence before we make these calls." Yusuf returned to his seat and sat down, crossing his legs, adjusting the crease in his pant leg just so, and looked up, smiling, apparently happy with the direction the conversation was going. "We know which banks are well run and have the ability to maintain through this crisis. We know everything there is to know about your bank and about you, J.R." Yusuf reached down and pulled a file from his briefcase. "Here's what we are suggesting. I think you are going to like this, J.R."

J.R. sank back into his chair again and rested his elbow on the desk, supporting his chin with his hand, and exhaled.

Yusuf continued, "Congress allocated seven hundred and fifty billion dollars through the T.A.R.P. program." He looked up from the file, smiled, and then returned to his notes.

J.R. said, with extreme lack of enthusiasm, "I know, I know."

"We are going to transfer to your treasury account about twenty million to start." Yusuf again looked up and smiled. "Before you start doing handstands and cart wheels, understand there are some strings attached. You will need to issue preferred stock representing twenty percent equity ownership as collateral, along with a warrant for an additional twenty thousand shares of common, if it should become necessary. Oh, yes, and we will need to be represented on your board, just one seat. Really, not much to ask, don't you agree?"

J.R. had allowed his thoughts to wander again, but the mention of the board brought him back. "What board? My board? My bank board? No way. We don't need your stinking twenty million, either."

This brought Yusuf to attention and he said, mimicking J.R. in a Hispanic twang, "We don't need no stinkin' twenty million— *Treasure of the Sierra Madre,* right? The Mexican guy talking to Humphrey Bogart at the end? I'm kind of an old movie buff."

J.R.'s face was blank.

"Okay, forget that, but I guess we are all set here. I'll have our legal department get hold of your legal counsel." He studied his file again. "Jones, Day, out of Chicago. You don't mess around do you, Mr. Roberts? They're top notch and very expensive." Yusuf put his files back in his briefcase, announcing the meeting was ending.

FIRST STATE BANK and (dis)TRUST of Hinkley County

"Wait a minute. Wait a minute. Don't you listen? I just told you we don't want anything to do with this. We don't want your money, and we—"

Yusuf rose from his chair, towering over the desk. "I'm sure you will change your mind once you have time to think about it. Good day, Mr. Roberts."

Yusuf turned, opened the door, put on a grand smile to greet Sally once again, and exited, leaving J.R. sitting with his mouth open.

Officer Jones

CHAPTER 5

Pucker stood at the bus stop anticipating the arrival of the nine o'clock shuttle to take him from the parking lot of the Cougar Falls Best Western to the Super Value in Hinkley. He had spent most of Saturday afternoon, after spending the morning manning the drive-through window at the bank, wandering aimlessly through the Cougar Falls mall counting the number of storefronts declaring going out of business sales. He then dined at the McDonald's across the street before concluding his day of shopping at the adult video store just across the city limit line near the Best Western.

The super-sized Coke he had consumed played havoc with his bladder and he knew he had to relieve himself before the shuttle bus arrived. His best bet for concealment was a patch of shrubs in the corner of the parking lot farthest from the light pole near the bus stop. He gathered his packages, not wanting anyone to abscond with his purchase, the newest release of Linda Lickidy Split in *My Account's in Arrears.*

FIRST STATE BANK and (dis)TRUST of Hinkley County

He stood with his back to the parking area behind a small bush staring up at the impending night sky and felt a shiver of relief. During his few seconds of assumed privacy a car made a fast turn into the lot and headed straight toward his bushy sanctuary. At the last second, the car swerved into a parking space well away from the building and any lighting. Pucker ducked down in midstream, soiling himself in the maneuver, trying frantically to stem the tide of urine.

He peeked over the shrub, holding himself and trying to decide his next move. Then recognition jolted him like a frayed extension cord. The person getting out of the Mercedes was Mr. Roberts, and he was humping at a fast pace toward the rear door of the motel. Pucker rose to a full standing position and was about to yell a greeting when he thought better of it, realizing there might be some explanation necessary, given his current state of disrepair. But his thought wheels kept turning. *Why would Mr. Roberts go in the back door of a motel just twenty miles from his home and park out back, away from the lights?*

Pucker slapped himself in the forehead. *Of course, it's some kind of hold-up, like in that movie where the bandits hold the bank president hostage and make him go to the bank, get the money, and then, then—what did they do then?* He squeezed his ears with both hands—a practice he imagined was developed by ancient shamans when they needed extra brain power to solve unanswered questions of the universe—or maybe it was just a habit he picked up as a child. Anyway, he squeezed with all his might. *Did they go back to the motel? I think they did. They held the bank guy all night and made him open the safe in the morning before anyone else got there. And he couldn't do anything because they were holding his family hostage somewhere else.*

"Holy Moses," Pucker whispered as he danced behind the bush trying to decide what to do. Then he thought he saw Mr. Roberts at a window on the ground floor just down from where he entered the building, pulling a drape shut.

Pucker knelt and tried to gather his thoughts. He could call the police, but there was not much time, and he would have to find a pay phone, and that was nearly impossible anymore.

He could go into the motel and warn the desk attendant, but that might cause some kind of standoff, and what about Mr. Roberts's family? No, he had to make sure his assumptions were correct and then devise a plan.

First, he would go to the window where he thought he saw Mr. Roberts and see if there was a way to see into the room so he could identify how many villains were guarding his boss. Once he established what he was up against, he could decide on a plan to save the bank.

He picked up his sack containing his videodisks and stealthily moved across the parking lot, swerving well beyond the light standards. Reaching the corner of the building, he crouched and slowly made his way along the wall, ducking below each window as he passed. When he reached the correct window, he sat down, drawing in long breaths, trying to calm himself. He imagined looking in the window and seeing the long barrel of Dirty Harry's revolver pointing right between his eyes.

Pucker decided to slowly raise himself to the point where there was some light streaming out of the window and take a quick look. If the situation was under control and he could count the number of occupants, it would be enough to confirm his suspicions.

But what if they were torturing Mr. Roberts, or worse yet, had killed him? Mr. Roberts was a man above men, strong and able to solve vast banking problems with a sweep of his hands, but this might be too much for even such a man as him. What then?

All he could do was take a quick look and try not to be seen. He slowly turned and, leaning on the wall below the window, began raising himself up, inch by inch, until he could just peek over the sill through a small crack in the drawn curtain.

He could not see much. There was some movement on the bed, but his vision was obscured, and he could only see two pairs of feet hanging over the end of the bed in a most unusual configuration. He strained to get a better look, but there was not enough separation in the curtain to see the rest of the bed. One good thing—he could not see any other people in the room.

FIRST STATE BANK and (dis)TRUST of Hinkley County

"Okay, Peeper, what in the he-ell you think you're doin' out here?" Officer Jones pinned the bright beam of his two-foot flashlight on Pucker's face. Then he shone the light on Pucker's pants, which were still wet. His fly was still open. "Jesus, you perverted nut wad, stand up," he bellowed. "Turn around, put your hands on the wall, and spread your legs. Damn, I left my gloves in the cruiser. Well, I ain't feelin' around in those trousers, I can tell you that, so you better not have nothin' illegal. You got a gun or knife or anything, peeper?"

"Officer, you've got to do something. I think they are holding the bank president hostage in there." Pucker motioned with his head toward the window he was peeking into to show Officer Jones where to look and to his astonishment, saw J.R. Roberts staring back at him, holding the curtain tight around his face, trying to cover the rest of his torso.

"Shut up. Why do I have to get every nut wad that walks the street? I gotta get on the day shift again," Jones said, pulling some wire ties from the pouch on his belt. "I suppose there are two-headed aliens in there, too, and they told you to pull your pud out here in the bushes, you sicko sum bitch," he muttered as he pulled the wire ties tight around Pucker's hands behind his back.

Pucker started to plead his case again but saw another face in the window. His jaw dropped as Sally Butterbetter stared back at him without the curtain drawn tight, exposing her bra and panty-clad body.

Officer Jones looked up, and after a second or two of trained police observation said, "Damn, will you look at those hooters. No wonder you were whackin' off in the bushes."

Sally smiled a wry smile and then yanked the curtain closed.

"Too bad for you, peeper; it still don't make it right. You can't go around peeking in windows, no matter how good the scenery is."

J.R. came out of the motel door and walked along the parking area, keeping his distance from Officer Jones and Pucker, but straining to get a better look at Pucker's face. After confirming that it was indeed Ernest Eisley that was handcuffed against the wall, he approached Officer Jones. "Uh, what seems to be the problem here, officer?"

Jones looked at Pucker and then at J.R. "It's kind of obvious, don't you think? He's a deviant, a freak. He likes to pull his pecker out in front of people. He likes to peek in windows, and what better place than a motel with lots of windows and lots of people to peek at."

Pucker finally saw an opportunity to defend himself. "I thought you were being kidnapped."

"Shut up, peeper. I told you before, and I won't tell you again," Jones led Pucker down the sidewalk toward the cruiser.

"But officer," J.R. interrupted, "here's the problem. I'm Jerome Roberts, president of the First State Bank over in Hinkley. If Peeper, I mean Ernest, was trying to prevent a crime of some sort, maybe even involving the bank, shouldn't we at least hear what he has to say? And if it involves the bank, I should hear it from him personally, in private."

Jones was getting irritated. "Look Mr. President, or whoever you are, the only privacy this loony is going to have until Monday is the back seat of the cruiser because once we get to the station, he's going into the tank with all the rest of the weekenders. Now, if you don't want to join him, I suggest you go back inside and go back to doin' whatever it was you were doin'."

J.R. watched the two men shuffle toward the front of the building. He was supposed to be in Chicago on his boat and had driven back for this rendezvous with Sally. Worse than that, Ernest obviously had some reason for being outside the window. J.R. thought, *He must know about his affair with Sally. Why else would he be at this motel at this time peeking in this exact window?*

J.R. reached for the door into the motel at the same time Sally reached from the inside. She allowed him to enter and said, "What was Pucker doing out there with the police? Where'd they go?"

"You mean Peeper, or Pee—Ernest?"

"No, I mean Pucker, the puke that works the teller line and likes to look up my dress. What was he doing in the parking lot with the police?"

Now J.R. was even more confused. "The cop called him Peeper, you call him Pucker, and I thought his name was Ernest. I don't know what he was doing in the parking lot, other than playing with himself while he looked in windows."

"What window? Our window? He was watching us? Did he see us doing it? Well, this ought to play well at the office." Sally walked back down the hall toward their room. When she reached the door, she turned and said, "I'd say you've got a big problem."

❖

Monday at ten A.M., Pucker was marched into the Cougar Falls Municipal Court for his hearing. He was fifth in line on the docket and sat stoic in the front row, waiting his turn. A public defender spoke to him just before he was marched into the courtroom and advised him to offer a no-contest plea since all of the charges were misdemeanors and would more than likely only result in fines. He further advised that the hearing was merely a formality.

The first four defendants were all drunk-driving offenses. All pleaded not guilty and were assigned future court dates after having their driving privileges suspended.

The magistrate who handled misdemeanor cases in lieu of a real elected judge, called for the next case, and his clerk read the charges. "Ernest E. Eisley; Indecent exposure, pandering, trespassing. Officer Jones of the C.F.P.D. is here to testify, if necessary, Your Honor. Mr. Eisley, step up to the defendant's podium, please."

Pucker slowly rose and stepped up to the podium, where the prior four defendants had been redressed. The magistrate coughed into the microphone, adjusted his reading glasses, and reviewed some papers that had been placed in front of him by the clerk.

"Mr. Eisley, these are serious charges. Even though they are misdemeanors, they carry serious penalties. Do you understand the charges?"

Pucker, reeking of urine and other bodily discharges found in the weekend drunk tank, raised his head, and with a quivering lip and a barely audible voice said, "I thought I was going to save the bank. I thought Mr. Roberts was kidnapped, like in the movie."

The magistrate looked at the clerk and rolled his eyes. "Okay, it sounds like we need Officer Jones to straighten this out. Call the witness."

The clerk called for Officer Jones, who was sworn in after giving his full name, rank, and badge number. The magistrate asked for his report.

"I received a call—" He checked his steno note pad. "At twenty o' seven from the dispatcher saying the motel had a peeper."

"They had a what?" the magistrate asked, turning and leaning toward Jones.

"A peeper looking in the windows. We get 'em every once in a while. Anyway, I responded, parked the cruiser out front, and walked the perimeter. Came around the back corner, the darkest part of the lot, and found old Mr. Eisley here peeking in a window, and you know." Officer Jones muttered something as the magistrate bent down, trying to hear.

"Speak up, Officer Jones. You saw him and what?"

Officer Jones looked at the magistrate and mouthed something.

"It's got to be on the record, Officer Jones. It has to be recorded on the tape so it can be transcribed. What did you see?"

Jones looked at the clerk, then at the defendants, family members, and miscellaneous on-lookers and bellowed, "He was floggin' the dog; he was spankin' the monkey; he was strokin' the sausage; he was—"

"Okay, okay, we get the picture."

"He was chokin' the chicken; he was—"

"I said that's enough, Jones." The magistrate pounded his fist on the oak throne, trying to quiet the crowd.

Officer Jones enjoyed his comedic reception and smiled, trying to think of a few more metaphors.

The magistrate pounded his fist one more time before looking back at Jones and saying, "Are you finished with the entertainment segment of your testimony, Officer Jones? Is there anything else you would like to add? And if there's any more barnyard humor, you'll be taking a week off without pay."

Jones cleared his throat, glanced at the magistrate, and said, "Well, nothing, I guess, other than he had a porn flick with him. I guess just in case he couldn't get it goin' in the parking lot, he'd always have a back up." Once again, the crowd burst into laughter, and Jones couldn't hide his pleasure.

"All right, get out of here, Jones; I've had enough." The magistrate waited for Jones to clear the witness stand before continuing. "Mr. Eisley, not a pretty picture. The only thing you've got going for you is that you have never been caught before. I'd say there's enough here to set a trial date if you wish to plead innocent. I am sure you have been advised there are two other choices. What's your pleasure, Mr. Eisley, innocent, guilty, or *no contende?*"

The room went silent, the courtroom audience waiting on the edge of their seats for his decision. Pucker stared at the magistrate, his mouth so dry he had difficulty getting it open, and no words formed. He tried, "Nnnnn-nnnn," but again, the words would not form.

"What was that, Mr. Eisley? What did you say? Speak up, Mr. Eisley. We have other cases to hear."

"N-n-no c-c-contest." As soon as he got the last syllable out, the room broke into applause, whistles, and catcalls.

The magistrate again pounded his fist in objection. "Quiet down, you morons; this isn't the *Jerry Springer Show*. Okay, Mr. Eisley, I think you said no contest. Am I correct?"

Pucker nodded.

"Then it's all done except for the sentencing. Do you understand that a no contest plea carries the same sentence as a guilty plea?"

Once again, Pucker nodded.

From the back of the room, someone raised a hand and shouted, "Your Honor, if I may, I would like to say something."

"It's a little late," the magistrate said, eyeing the smartly dressed man, "but come on up here; it can't get any worse."

J.R. had been sitting in the back of the courtroom next to a weeping woman—Pucker's mother, although J.R. was not aware of it—and had listened to the proceeding, cringing at the lurid descriptions and pondering if he had made the correct decision to attend. When the magistrate signaled the finality of the hearing, he felt compelled to speak. Now that he had been recognized, he wasn't sure it was a smart decision.

"My name is Jerome Roberts. I am Mr. Eisley's employer and the president of the First State Bank and Trust of Hinkley. I feel compelled to offer comments regarding Mr. Eisley's work habits, I guess. We regard our employees as part of our family and—"

"Okay, I get the picture," the magistrate interrupted. "Given the situation and what we have heard, you may want to re-evaluate your hiring practices, but that's none of the court's business and isn't relevant. In thirty seconds or less, tell us about the defendant's work habits, and if it has anything to do with bathrooms or barnyards, I strongly suggest you skip it."

J.R. hesitated and thought about just turning around and exiting, leaving Ernest to suffer the consequences on his own. Then he thought about dividing his bank stock down the middle due to a nasty divorce and said, "Ernest has worked for the bank for over five years. He is dedicated, has never missed a day or been tardy, and has never shown signs of any sexually deviant behavior. We have never had a complaint. Now, with regard to the incident in question—"

"Mr. Roberts, the incident is no longer in question. The defendant has said he was there and, although without admission, did what the officer said he did."

Someone in the back of the courtroom yelled, "Choked his chicken."

The magistrate rose from his chair and scanned the assembly. "If I hear one more outburst from any of you, there will be no more innocent pleas taken today. Do I make myself clear?" The room quieted. He remained standing, towering over

FIRST STATE BANK and (dis)TRUST of Hinkley County

the courtroom, and with a look of disgust stared at J.R. "You have anything else to add, Mr. Roberts?"

"Uh, I guess not." J.R. bowed as he backed away from the bench.

"Okay, can we get this over with?" the magistrate said as he settled back in his chair, looking at his clerk and then at Pucker. "Ernest Eisley? Stand up, Ernest. Given the severity of the offense and," he hesitated, looking to the back of the courtroom at J.R., who was standing near the exit door, "considering your exemplary employment record, I am dismissing the trespassing charge since it was a public place; I am dismissing the pandering charge, since Officer Jones, during his standup routine, failed to mention anything to do with pandering. You are found guilty of indecent exposure in a public place and are sentenced to two days jail, time served and two years probation, and during such time, if there is another incident, you will be subject to the sex offender statute if the offense permits and may be required to register as a sex crime offender. Oh, and a five hundred-dollar fine, including costs. Do I make myself clear, Mr. Eisley? Do you understand?"

Pucker turned and looked at J.R. still standing at the back of the room, smiled bleakly, turned back to the magistrate, straightened, and as if he were accepting marital vows in the National Cathedral said boldly, "I do."

Pucker was ushered out of the courtroom through the clerk's exit and stood in another line waiting to be processed at the clerk's counter. When he finally reached the head of the line, the clerk's assistant asked without looking up, "Name?"

"Ernest Eisley."

"Your term of probation starts immediately and will last for two years. The only restriction is that you do not show your face here or in any other courtroom for this type of offense again. Your fine is five hundred dollars. We take Visa, Master Card, debit card, personal check, or cash. If the check comes back, it's a violation of your probation, and you will be in contempt of court and subject to arrest, do you understand?" The assistant did not look up from her notes. "How do you intend to pay?"

"I will take care of that." J.R. slid through the crowd, trying not to touch any of the other violators waiting in line. He pushed five one hundred-dollar bills into Pucker's hand and without comment turned and headed for the door.

"Hey, bro, how about throwin' some of that jack my way?" one of the offenders said as J.R. moved by. "My old lady is sick, man, can't even feed my damn dog. A Ulysses S. Grant would do me just fine. You wouldn't even miss it, man. Shit, man, your socks cost more than that." Now the whole line started in on J.R.

One woman who had been arrested for solicitation said, "What he have to do to get you to pay his thang? I'll do it twice as good, honey, and make you come back beggin' for more." There were some whistles and a couple "yeah, momma" and "who yo daddy."

"Hey, man, don't leave," another line patron said. "You all need any more help down at the bank? I be 'sperienced, man. I did a nickel for passin' bad paper a few years back; I know a lot 'bout bankin'." The crowd burst out laughing as J.R. rushed through the exit door.

❖

Pucker bumped through the exit door, apprehensive and tentative, and looked up and down the hallway for J.R. Far down the hall, near the foyer, he saw the silhouette of someone half-hidden by a bulletin board on an easel. The person peeked around the sign and motioned for Pucker to approach.

Pucker walked up the hall and, not knowing what to say, held out his hand to offer thanks for Mr. Roberts's generosity.

"Don't touch me," J.R. said in disgust. "For Christ's sake, Ernest, you smell like a sewer."

Pucker looked down, examining his soiled pants and crumpled shirt. "I-I didn't, couldn't clean up. They wouldn't let me use the bathroom before court."

"All right, forget it for now. Ernest, I want to know what you were doing in that parking lot—looking in my window."

Pucker started to open his mouth, but during the few seconds he used to gather his thoughts, his mother came around

FIRST STATE BANK and (dis)TRUST of Hinkley County

the corner of the hall, waddling as fast as her size tens would take her, arms open, tears streaming down her face. "Oh, Ernest, my poor baby. Oh, Ernest, what have they done to you?" She hugged him, sobbing, "Oh, Ernest, my poor baby."

J.R. crossed his arms impatiently, looking around the expansive hallway, hoping no one else he knew noticed their encounter. "Mrs. Eisley, would you mind if I talked to Ernest alone for a moment?"

Mrs. Eisley turned, and through her red, bulging eyes and thick, red lipstick-encrusted mouth exclaimed, "Oh, Mr. Roberts, God bless you." She reached for him, and he threw his hands up just in time to ward off her hug and her huge red lips. Her advance pushed him against the near wall, and he had no defense other than hand-to-hand combat.

"Mrs. Eisley, please," he said, trying to hold her back. She blubbered something he could not interpret and a large gob of drool sprouted from her clown-sized lips, joining the tears streaming down her face. "Oh, my God," was all he said as he envisioned that drool and those lips meeting the lapel of his new sports coat. He continued to grab at her reaching hands. "Ernest, Ernest, tell her to get back." J.R. glanced at Pucker, who stood motionless, his mouth open, staring in trancelike silence. J.R. pleaded with greater authority, "Ernest, tell her to stop this, right now."

The bite in his voice seemed to quell Mrs. Eisley's advance enough for him to feint left before making a quick move to his right. Mrs. Eisley reached at nothing and stumbled into the wall, leaving a big smear of red lipstick on the yellowing ceramic tile. She emitted a loud grunt and passed what sounded like an enormous amount of gas, although through what orifice, J.R. could not determine.

They stood silently looking at Mrs. Eisley as she turned from the wall, her face contorted and awash with smeared lipstick and saliva. "Mother, this is Mr. Roberts, the bank president. Mr. Roberts, this is my mother, Edna Eisley," Pucker said in a formal tone.

Edna started to raise her hands again, and J.R. jumped back, raising his own hands and bending his knees, preparing for another evasive move. "Nice to meet you," he said tentatively and then spoke to Ernest, keeping his attention on Edna. "Ernest, we need to talk alone for a minute. Do you suppose you could get your mother to go wait in the car? Mrs. Eisley, Ernest and I need to talk about some bank issues. You understand, don't you? It will just take a minute, and then Ernest will be able to go home, and we can forget about this, this—incident," he hesitated, looking for the appropriate word. "He can even take a couple days off to recover."

Edna snorted, clearing her nostrils, pushed her lacquered hair off her forehead, sobbed, and then hobbled toward the exit door, not looking back. Pucker raised his hand and gave a slight wave. "I'll be right there, Mother."

J.R. looked over his shoulder again, checking the hall, making sure they were alone, and then turned his attention to Pucker, towering over him. "All right, Ernest, once again, what in the name of God were you doing at that motel looking in my window? And don't give me any lame story like you tried to tell the judge. I want to know what you know and what you saw—got it?"

Pucker tried to stand a little taller and gather his thoughts. "Well, I had gone to Cougar Falls for my usual—"

"How did you know about Sally and me, huh? You little weasel—did you follow me there? Wait, you couldn't have followed me. I didn't come from home. Somehow, you found out ahead of time, didn't you? You l-l-little rat. And th-th-then y-you watch us and wh-wh-whack off in the bushes?"

J.R. stopped, tried to calm himself, rubbed his forehead, and realized he was sweating profusely. He drew in a couple of long breaths, closed his eyes, waited for the pounding in his skull to subside, and said, "What is it you want? Is it money? You think you can get rich off me? Well, forget it. All I have to do is spread it around that you are a pervert, and you won't be able to walk down the street in Hinkley without being pounded into the sidewalk. You little weasel, I step on pissants like you and keep

FIRST STATE BANK and (dis)TRUST of Hinkley County

walking." J.R. looked toward the door and noticed a group of pedestrians walking toward the entrance. He rubbed his forehead again, gave Pucker a stern look, and whispered, "This isn't over. We are going to finish this at the bank, understood?"

HINKLEY MESSENGER: JUNE 12, 2009
EXHIBITIONIST ARRESTED
Cougar Falls:

Local resident Ernest Eisley, age 28, was arrested Saturday night at the Cougar Falls Best Western motel and charged with indecent exposure, trespassing, and pandering. The police report indicates Eisley was apprehended while peeking in windows of occupied motel rooms and exposing himself. Eisley later pled no contest to the indecent exposure charge and the remaining charges were dropped as part of the plea agreement. Eisley received 2 days jail and a $500 fine.

Eisley is employed by the First State Bank and Trust Company of Hinkley County. State criminal records indicate this is his only arrest in Illinois.

Sally Butterbetter

CHAPTER 6

Sally looked up when J.R. entered the bank dressed in a sports coat and loafers, unusually casual for a work day. He briskly walked past her into his office and slammed the door. With the exception of Sally, not one employee looked up or acknowledged his entrance. Sally pushed some papers around on her desk, stood, adjusted her skirt, brushed imaginary lint from her silk sleeve, turned, walked to J.R.'s office, and entered without knocking.

J.R. sat at his desk, apparently studying an adjacent wall adorned with numerous pictures of him with political dignitaries. He did not acknowledge Sally's entrance.

She reported, "The bank examiners are here. They are in the basement with John and Betty reviewing stuff. Adam Buckminster from Jones Day called and said you need to call him a.s.a.p. He said he called your cell and it was off. And…" she said, letting the statement linger, "Pucker the peeper didn't show up for work today. Imagine that."

FIRST STATE BANK and (dis)TRUST of Hinkley County

"Are we referring to Ernest Eisley?" J.R. said without looking at Sally.

"He's the only Pucker the peeper I know," Sally replied with a chuckle.

J.R. turned with smoldering fire in his eyes. "You think this is funny? You think this is some kind of joke Ernest was playing? Well, it's not, and I would suggest you start considering things like that new convertible you drive and those clothes you wear, not to mention the check you take home every week. All of that could easily go out the window if, what did you call him, 'Pucker the peeper' decides to make things nasty for me. How do you think he knew about the Best Western?" J.R.'s questions drew silence. "It sure didn't come from me. I couldn't have picked Eisley out of a lineup until he showed up outside that window."

The accusatory tone made her smile disappear and the quivering lip syndrome start.

"Sorry, but that isn't going to work this time. This is too serious for me to overlook. Are you telling me you have never talked to him or anyone about us meeting at the Best Western?"

Sally slumped down in the chair in front of the desk. "You think I'm nuts? You think I go around talking to perverts like him? Give me a break, J.R. Who would I talk to in this bank? Greta the gargantuan Smith who comes to work with cow manure on her shoes? Or maybe Mary Snider who teaches Sunday school at my father's church? Yeah, we could talk about my affair with you and maybe compare notes. Hell, she might be shacking up with my dad at the same motel."

"Keep your voice down," J.R. said in a loud whisper, waving his hand and pointing at the door. "Okay, I get your point, but he had to have some motive other than just wanting to spy on us."

"Maybe he's doin' it with your wife and she sent him to spy on us," Sally said with a childish smirk, then saw J.R.'s face redden and quickly added, "then again, maybe not."

J.R. opened his mouth to reprimand Sally for the remark, but was interrupted by his intercom speakerphone. "Mr. Roberts, excuse me for interrupting, but Miss Butterbetter is not at her desk again." There was a lingering pause emphasizing the reported absense. "And Mr. Buckminster from Jones Day is on line four and says it is urgent that he talk to you."

"Okay, okay, I'll take the call." He looked at Sally as he picked up the receiver, assuming she would understand and leave his office. Instead, she adjusted her bra strap and crossed her legs, settling in for the duration of the call. "Addy, nice of you to call. What's on your mind that's so important?" he said, swiveling his chair and turning his back to Sally.

Adam Buckminster, the bank's business counsel and J.R.'s personal attorney had a small investment in the bank along with his large retainer. "J.R., what's going on down there? You guys in trouble? I thought you would have at least let me know so I could dump my stock. I'm your attorney."

"What, you didn't get your dividend check? It mailed out last week."

"No, I got it, but there's a treasury department attorney coming here today. Something about your loan from the government and wanting to give me protocol for issuing preferred stock in the bank. You guys need to be bailed out? Hey, that reminds me. You know that personal loan we did for my place in Wisconsin? If you guys go down or they sell you to another bank, will that loan go away? I mean, it was never recorded, was it? It could be buried in a bottom drawer along with the rest of the misplaced paperwork, couldn't it?"

"We're not going away or being sold, and your loan's not going away, either," J.R. responded. "And nobody's getting any preferred stock, except maybe my wife," he said, glaring at Sally's reflection in the window behind his chair as she fidgeted with her pleated skirt.

"I'm lost here, J.R. You need to explain this to me. Preferred stock for your wife? And this government guy—it didn't sound like this was a matter of choice to me; it sounded more like a done deal."

J.R. rubbed his forehead in disgust, turned, and looked at Sally, who had pulled a small mirror from somewhere and was meticulously adjusting her lipstick. "Uh, could you get me a cup of coffee or something?"

Sally expressed her newfound self-confidence by taking a lengthy moment to return the mirror and lipstick to a hidden pocket, adjusting her blouse, then standing and straightening her skirt, the whole time holding her gaze on J.R. She turned, slowly walked to the door, and exited without looking back. He held his head, resting his elbows on the desk, and said, "Forget about what I said about my wife; it's just some issues that will be resolved."

"She didn't find out about that pretty young thing you brought up to my cottage, did she? That could get expensive J.R., not to mention the legal fees," Buckminster said in jest, but then realized after a long silence he had touched a sore nerve. "Well, anyway, this guy should be coming up the elevator any minute. Let me find the note. Let's see—Armando Vasquez, special counsel to the Department of the Treasury. Ever heard of him?"

"Of course I've never heard of him. I've never heard of any of these maggots feeding off the public trough."

"Let's not get bitter, J.R. These guys are pretty high up on the food chain, and you might get eaten. Wait a minute. He's here. I just got a headline on my monitor to come to the reception desk. Well, it's show time. What do you want me to tell him? Are we going to play ball?"

J.R. growled something unintelligible and then said, "Just talk to him and then call me. Don't commit to anything. I need to make some calls to Washington and our state banking association lobbyist." He hung up the phone and leaned back in his chair, exhausted. It was only eleven in the morning.

The intercom chirped, and Sally said, "Mrs. Roberts is on the phone for you, and she seems more unhappy than usual for so early in the morning."

He carefully picked up the receiver and punched the blinking button. "Yes, dear, what—"

"What were you doing in court in Cougar Falls this morning? Maureen Kubinski called and said her son was in court this morning for some minor traffic ticket or something and said she saw you sitting in the courtroom waiting your turn. She had to leave to get Frankie back to school, but said everyone else there was being hit with drunk-driving fines. Were you picked up again and, my God, in Cougar Falls? You can't get drunk in your own town? You self-righteous bag of wind, you don't want your customers to see you out carousing with those flirts you call friends. Is that it, J.R.? Or was it a more serious charge this time? Going to do time?"

J.R. took a moment to gather his thoughts. His response needed to be creative, but honest; authoritative, but sincere; lack respect, yet be condescending.

"Well, Monica, since you are making this your business, I guess an explanation is necessary, if for no other reason than to let me get back to running this bank. One of our employees found himself in a little difficulty over the weekend and ended up in the Cougar Falls jail. There was some misunderstanding about the charges, and I felt I needed to supply the court with employment history prior to any sentencing." He heard Monica breathing on the other end of the line, apparently carefully considering her next inquiry.

"Who is this employee that you are so concerned about?"

"Really, dear, I don't think we need to go any further with this. Just leave it alone and understand that our employees are important to us. It's my job to make sure they are not getting in trouble, and if they do, that it's not anything serious." He leaned back in the chair, content with his explanation.

There was continued silence, punctuated by an occasional heavy breath. "Was it a female?"

Now he could quash this conversation and stay on the high ground. "Once again, let's just drop this, okay? If you must know, it was not a female. I have examiners in the building and our attorney on the other line. I've got to go, and please, don't mention this to anyone; it is confidential bank business that I have shared with you but no one else, understood?" The line went dead without response.

John White

Chapter 7

John White knocked lightly on J.R.'s office door, looking over his shoulder as if he was on some clandestine mission. As a rule, he was not seen on the main floor of the bank, his position as vice president of finance confining him to an obscure office on the second floor surrounded by computer monitors and stacks of continuous feed computer paper. He was about to knock again when the door swept open and J.R. almost ran over him exiting the office. Barely avoiding a head butt, J.R. said, "What the— What are you doing out here?" Since the encounter with Ernest, his suspicion meter was on high alert.

"Mr. Roberts," John looked over his shoulder, wary of anyone within earshot, and said in a conspiratorial whisper, "we just received a wire transfer from the Federal Home Loan Bank—you know, the feds."

J.R. looked at him with disinterested anticipation. "So what? And why are you whispering?" He looked around the lobby, noted that Sally, as usual, was not at her desk, but found no one close enough to hear their conversation. "Seriously, John, I don't have time for this right now. Go back to your office or harass the examiners for a while."

"But Mr. Roberts, you don't understand. This wasn't just any wire transfer, like a mortgage reimbursement or something; this was a, a—"

After expelling a long breath, J.R. said, "A what, John? Spit it out; I don't have all day." He really wasn't listening to what John was saying; he was thinking about jettisoning the balance of the day's schedule and playing golf instead.

"It's, it's, …… twenty million dollars. That's seven zeros and a two. I counted them. Plop, right into our account. I suppose it's a mistake, like the time they accidently added the two zeros to our interest payment." He looked over his shoulder and around the room. "But even so, I rolled it into the overnight treasury account. We could make a little over sixty-five hundred dollars interest in the next forty-eight hours, assuming they don't find the error and call us on it. I suppose we could just ignore them for today; you know, not answer the e-mails." John beamed, expecting a sound congratulatory slap on the back. "You think they'll make us give it back—the interest—once they realize the mistake?"

J.R. watched Sally stroll across the lobby, returning to her desk after an extended break in the employee lounge. She stopped at her desk, picked up a penciled note, and took the few additional steps to intercede in their conversation.

Before she could speak, John took one of the rare opportunities he had to converse with her. "Hello, Sally, don't you look stunning today. Just like you stepped out of a magazine—a magazine, I tell you. Isn't that right, Mr. Roberts? Right out of a magazine." John was smiling like it was high school prom night and he was about to make the big score when he looked at J.R. and noted he did not share his delight; in fact, the crimson color of his face revealed he was either quite upset or on the verge of a coronary.

Sally interrupted, "Thank you, John; I'm surprised you noticed. Why, these old things; they're almost thread bare."

"All right, that's enough," J.R. said with disgust. "What do you want, Sally? We're busy here." And then, as if all else in the room, including Sally, froze in time, he turned to John, grasping his shoulders, staring straight into his eyes and said, "You said what? T-t-twenty m-m-million?" J.R.'s breathing was so intense it ruffled John's Dutch-boy bangs. He was so intimidated by the grasping hands and J.R.'s stuttering, his mouth fell open, but no words formed.

Sally, standing nearby said, "Maybe y-y-you guys ought to go back in the office." She then turned on her tiptoes and started back to her desk, but hesitated, stopped, and said, "Oh, I almost forgot. Adam Buckminster called again and said—" She referred to her scribbled note. "'Everything is a go with the feds,' whatever that means."

J.R. grasped White's shoulders so tightly the accountant began to whimper and squirm, trying to loosen the hold. "I'm sure it's just a mistake, Mr. Roberts, or maybe I misread it. Let me go, and I'll check again."

J.R. realized he may have been a little aggressive and released his hold, but guided the young man into his office and slammed the door. "You're telling me that twenty mil dropped into our account this morning?"

"Well, yeah, that's what I think happened. I mean, I'm sure it happened because I already transferred it to our overnight treasury account. Like I said, it's probably a mistake, but we stand to gain if they don't call us on the interest. Of course they are going to eventually find the mistaken deposit."

J.R. walked around his desk and leaned on his chair, staring out the window. "It's not a mistake. Well, at least it's not a mistake on their part."

After the episode outside the office door and J.R.'s monotone acceptance of the facts, White questioned J.R.'s mental state. Maybe the pressure of running the bank and, if the rampant rumors about his affair with Sally were true, his guilt had put him over the edge. During the few seconds of silence, White envisioned himself installed as president by the board, taking over for the mentally incompetent, broken down administrator.

FIRST STATE BANK and (dis)TRUST of Hinkley County

White's pipedream was shattered as quickly as it sprouted when J.R. said, "All right, get out of here. Don't mention this to anyone. I need some issues clarified before we make any decisions regarding distribution of the funds." J.R. sat in his chair. "Before you go back to your office, go downstairs and find out what the examiners are doing. They weren't scheduled to be here. Find out what they are looking for or what they have found and report back to me." J.R. picked up his phone and started to peck a number. He looked up, and White still stood in front of him, somewhat disheveled from the incident with a stunned expression. "And you are still standing here why?"

"Addy, what's going on? I told you not to do anything until I got back to you." J.R. held his head with his hand, leaned on the desk, and thought, *Could this day get any worse?*

"I didn't have any choice. They just waltzed in here, said you had directed them to get the show going, and said that the money had already been transferred to the bank's account. Said once the money was transferred, it was a done deal," Buckminster said with trepidation knowing he had acted without authority. "J.R., you just can't tell these guys no; they're the government."

"How do I get out of this? Do I just wire the money back?"

Buckminster's hesitation was evidence that he did not know the answer.

"Does anyone in that plush office have any answers, or do I need to find another firm with experience in this sort of thing?"

The threat brought Buckminster to attention. "It's not a matter of experience, J.R. No one has experience with this sort of thing. These people are making up the rules as they go, and everyone else is just following along, trying to read the thousands of pages of regulations as they spit out of the printer. My suggestion is that you wait until this week's board meeting and have a firm conversation with whomever they send as a representative."

"Board meeting? Representative? What are you talking about?"

"The seat on the board; that's part of the deal."

J.R. stood up so quickly his chair tipped backwards,

crashing against the credenza in front of the window. "What deal?" he screamed into the phone. "We have no deal. Do you understand? We have no deal. There is no deal. No deal." Sally peeked through the door after hearing the crash, started to open her mouth to ask what happened, and J.R. screamed, "G-g-get out of here."

BitterQuince

Chapter 8

The mid-day crowd at Ralphy's was sparse, with a few hard-core drinkers occupying stools at the bar and some lingering lunch patrons sitting in booths along the opposite wall. The front door was propped open, allowing the late summer breeze to filter in along with noise from an occasional honking horn or louder than normal muffler as the traffic made its way down Main Street.

Roger Witherspoon, a local barrister from the firm of Witherspoon and Witherspoon, which occupied an office next to the bar, sat on the end stool exchanging worthless, time-consuming comments with Ralphy, the establishment's owner.

"The Sox blew another one in the ninth last night. Seriously, it's like misery to watch them play anymore. Even worse, I had a fin on the game because they're playing Texas, the worst of the worst, in last place, and they still lose."

Ralphy stood behind the bar, his foot up on a box, an elbow propping his apron-clad stocky body up, and replied, "Don't you ever learn? It's the same thing every week. You bitch about the Sox, but then go bet on them to win. In the broad spectrum of logical thinking, which we both know is not your forte—wouldn't it make more sense to bet against them? Then when they win, at least you can have some comfort in the fact that your team won, even though you lost." Ralphy took his elbow off the bar, gave some thought to what he had just said and smiled. Even though he was just babbling, it had made some sense for a change.

"You hear about the Eisley kid?" Witherspoon asked, lowering his voice.

"You talking about Edna's kid; the one that always wears a tie with matching socks? He's a piece of work, for sure. I heard he might be, you know—" Ralphy looked down the bar to see if anyone was listening. "A peter puffer."

Witherspoon broke into a laugh. "A what?"

"You know what I mean—a rump ranger."

Witherspoon slapped his hand on the bar. "Where do you come up with this stuff? I haven't heard anyone use those names since I was in law school. You got to get a little more politically correct, Ralph; this is the twenty-first century. Anyway, the way I heard it from the assistant prosecutor over in the Falls—he got caught peeking in windows at the Best Western. And that's not the best part. Listen to this. They caught him jerkin' off while he was doin' it."

Ralphy took a step back from the bar and said, "You've got to be joking. What'd they arrest him for, playin' pocket pool in a public place?" Both men had trouble talking through their laughter. "Poor Ernest. Kind of got himself in a sticky situation."

Witherspoon rocked on the bar stool holding his stomach and laughing so hard he nearly lost his balance.

Ralphy abruptly stopped laughing, although the attempt made him cover his mouth and act as if he was coughing as another bar patron walked through the open door. The man was tall, at least six feet or better, his height accentuated by his heeled cowboy boots and the Stetson he had tilted on his head. His chiseled features reminded Ralphy of a movie star, although he couldn't place the name. His neatly pressed pants, well-tailored sports coat, and open shirt collar gave further evidence of wealth and importance.

He approached the bar and stood next to Witherspoon, one boot resting on the foot rail as he gently placed his Stetson on the stool next to him. "How you all doin'? I could sure use a cold one. I got a dry gulch thirst that may take some time to satisfy. My name's Quince, Bitter Quince. Friends just call me Bit."

"Well, Bit, you look like a longneck man to me. Any preference?" Ralphy slid down the bar toward the cooler.

"Whatever's cold will do. When you got a hankerin' for a cold one, you can't be choosy."

Ralphy slid the longneck down the bar, followed it back to his box, and rested his foot. "Need a glass?"

"No, this is gonna do me just fine. Don't get too comfortable; I'm gonna need another here real soon." Bit took a long draw on the longneck. "Oh, man, that's good. You know, there's just times when nothing else'll do except a cold beer."

"You new around here?" Ralphy asked. "Can't say I've seen you before. Small town, you know, not that I'm nosy or anything, but we don't see that many new faces in here."

Witherspoon leaned back on his stool and looked at Bit as if he was about to participate in the inquisition, but instead hooked his thumb through his suspender and waited for Bit's answer.

Bit took another long draw on his beer and relaxed, obviously in no hurry to explain his intentions. After exhausting a long breath, as if he had just received a reprieve from a death sentence, he said, "Man, that tastes good. I told you not to get too comfortable." Ralphy marched back down the bar and retrieved another bottle. Bit looked around the bar and said, "How's the economy around here? Bad as the rest of the country?"

Witherspoon spoke up for the first time. "Things could be better. The latex factory, they made all kinds of stuff—gloves, you know, like they use in the hospital, and a bunch of other stuff... used to make rubbers, too—it moved to Mexico. Used to be a big anhydrous ammonia plant, too, now it's cheaper to process it in Mexico and bring it up the river by barge. The agriculture around here is still going, but the big factory farms are running the family farms out of business. So, to answer your question, things pretty much suck, just like the rest of the country."

Ralphy joined in, glad to have some variety in the afternoon bar talk. "Used to be I'd make a good living out of this place. Raised my family and sent two kids to college running this bar. Nowadays, can't hardly pay the bills. They opened an Applebug, or Applebee or something, out yonder by the Wal-Mart; my business dropped off thirty percent. Then the state came along and said that if anyone gets drunk in here and I don't take 'em home or call the sheriff, they can sue me for everything I got. It's a damn shame."

"I drove around a little," Bit said. "Looks like a real nice town—homey, if you know what I mean. Kinda reminds me of where I grew up—Logansville, Kansas. Had a bank, a bar, a school, five churches, and everyone had cow manure on their boots. Kids could go out at night, and the parents didn't have to worry about never seein' 'em again, stuff like that. You all have any problems like that around here?"

"Not really," Ralphy replied. "We were just talkin' about one of the locals gettin' caught peekin' in windows, but he's just an odd one, if you know what I mean." Ralphy rolled his eyes, thinking about Witherspoon's politically correct comment. "We've got a good sheriff and good people, for the most part. I mean, what are they gonna do except maybe get a little drunk and wreck their car? Might pass a bad check or two, but nothing too severe." He Looked at Witherspoon. "Roger, there been anything bad happen around here lately, like a robbery or anything?"

"No, if there was anything, I would know. I defend most of the crimes that get prosecuted around here." He pulled out a card and slid it toward Bit. "Roger Witherspoon, attorney; my office is right next door."

Bit let the card lie on the bar. "Damn, that beer goes down smooth." Ralphy and Witherspoon sat silently anticipating Bit's commentary on their town. Instead, Bit downed the last swig, set the empty bottle back on the bar, and reached into his pocket, pulling out a substantial roll of cash bound by a stout rubber band. He thumbed through what seemed like endless one hundred-dollar bills until he found a five, placed it on the bar, and rose, picking up his hat. "Well, boys, it's been a pleasure."

Not satisfied with the apparent conclusion of their conversation, Witherspoon inquired, "So, what's your business in Hinkley?"

"Just passin' through for the most part. Got a list of communities that interest me and this is one of them."

"Interested in what?" Witherspoon persisted.

Bit gave him a long look. "Investment. Just doing a little leg work."

"Investment in what?" asked Ralphy.

"Now, you boys are pushin' a little hard, aren't you? Man stops for a beer and he's got to explain his life plan." Bit let the hard comment float for a second. "Okay, no hard feelin's. Let's just say this is a nice community, and maybe, just maybe, I might be interested in doin' some business here."

Ralphy and Witherspoon looked at each other, knowing the next question needed to be asked but not wanting to be the one to do it.

Witherspoon relented. "What kind of business would that be, if you don't mind me asking? I mean, it's none of my business, but it's a small town, and when someone new comes around looking for information, it makes us curious."

Bit leaned against the bar and rested his hat again, sighing in resignation. "I do lots of things, but right now, the taste in my mouth says motel, the kind that gives folks a place to go and forget about their troubles. Pool, fancy restaurant, maybe even one of those water parks with the slides and such. You all don't have nothin' like that around here now, do you? Didn't see anything of the like when I drove around." He looked at the two staring back at him, and they both just shook their heads. "See? That's what I do; I look for opportunities where other people just see towns. Well, boys, it's sure been nice conversing with you. Now, keep that under your hats, will you? I don't want a bunch of people calling and asking about gettin' jobs and stuff. This is all in the wind, so to speak."

He picked up his hat, looked in the mirror behind the bar as he placed it just right on his head, tipped it with his finger in salutation, and headed for the door. Passing a couple sitting in a booth near the door, he smiled and said, "How you all doin' today?"

Bit walked into the sunshine, took a moment to let his eyes adjust, and then walked across the street and got in his Escalade, which was decked out with gold trim and gigantic chrome wheels. From inside the dark-tinted windows of the car, he saw Ralphy and Witherspoon peeking out the bar's front door. Bit smiled and said to himself, "By tonight, half the people in this town will be talkin' about a new motel and water park."

CHAPTER 9

J.R. followed his regular routine, having lunch at the club in advance of the night's board meeting. The only difference was that he had to forgo writing the minutes of the meeting since they would have a guest. He drafted the agenda and made detailed notes, giving himself and any other board members little latitude to stray. He just wanted to start the meeting, bring the motion to the floor to return the T.A.R.P. money, and then pose the question of allowing a government person to be on the board. He had already talked to everyone except Ralph Bellows, whom he could not find. He assumed he was in a bar somewhere. J.R. advised them to just follow his lead and vote to endorse the motion. He would then ask the intruder to leave, and that would be that.

Yusuf Olajuwon left a message at the bank that he would attend the meeting, and Sally courteously gave him directions to the club.

FIRST STATE BANK and (dis)TRUST of Hinkley County

J.R. instructed Miranda, the club dining room attendant, to have Mr. Olajuwon wait in the lobby until he was called into the meeting.

All of the board members were present and surrounded the large conference table, except Ralph Bellows, who had been conspicuously absent from the club bar all afternoon.

J.R. started the meeting with stern reproach. "As I told you all this afternoon, we will have a guest tonight, and it is extremely important that everyone keep quiet and act in an orderly fashion. This won't take long. We will just have the votes we discussed and get him out of here. Anyone have any questions, and does anyone know where Ralph is?"

Before anyone could answer, the large double doors swung open, and Miranda said, "Mr. Roberts, your guest is—"

Yusuf followed close behind her, a big smile on his face, his massive presence taking up a large portion of the opening. All of the seated board members stared in awe as the big man moved around the table and took the seat opposite J.R. at the other end of the long table. He sat his briefcase down, took out a laptop, opened it, and smiled.

"Thanks for inviting me this evening. My name is Yusuf Hussein Olajuwon. I represent the United States Department of Treasury and will be advising you during this and future board meetings. We will also provide support directly to the bank through our on-line support staff in our Chicago office."

"Whoa, slow down a minute there, Hussein," J.R. interrupted. "I don't know how many board meetings you have attended, but we don't just sit around and talk, or listen to anyone that walks in off the street. You want the floor, ask for it, but only after we have concluded our formal agenda. Before you burst in here, we had a motion on the floor, brought by, let's see, Mr. Lee. Let me read it back before I ask for a second. That motion is to send the money provided without authorization from the T.A.R.P. program back to the treasury. Do I have a second?"

Fred Chin Lee was still staring at the huge black man in the silk suit sitting at the end of the table when his name was mentioned. He turned to J.R. and said, "I didn't make—"

J.R. interrupted, "Once again, I am asking for a second to the motion."

Everyone stared at Yusuf.

"Father Tom, did I hear you say you second the motion?"

Father Tom turned to J.R. and said, "What money?"

"Was that a second? Any discussion?"

The double doors flew open, and Ralph Bellows staggered in holding a drink in his hand, smiling. "Better late than never. Sorry, but Martha worked me in the garden all day like a runaway nigra slave. My knees are swelled up like punkin's."

Silence enveloped the room as widened eyes moved from Ralph to Yusuf. Ralph followed their lead, looked at the far end of the table, and saw Yusuf sitting with both hands folded in front of him, a modest smile holding firm as he said, "Perhaps another introduction is in order. My name is Yusuf Hussein Olajuwon, here representing the United States Department of the Treasury. I don't believe I've had the pleasure of your acquaintance."

Ralph looked stunned, although it was difficult to recognize any blush in his already reddish complexion. "Who from where?" he babbled while he moved to take a seat as far from Yusuf as possible. He looked at J.R., who was glaring at him, and held his hand to his mouth whispering, "Uh, who is that? Is this a holdup or something? What's he doin' in here? I thought, you know, they weren't allowed in this club."

"Shut up, Ralph," J.R. said under his breath. "Now that the entire board is present, we will vote on the motion on the floor. All in favor say aye."

"Ah, Mr. Roberts," Yusuf said in a casual tone, "don't you think your board should discuss the issue before you vote? Have you considered the consequences of returning the T.A.R.P. funds?"

All of the heads that were turned toward Yusuf turned back to J.R., as if they were watching a slow-motion tennis match.

J.R. said, "I think we are in position to make a decision on this. I am confident this board will do what's right for the bank and its stockholders."

FIRST STATE BANK and (dis)TRUST of Hinkley County

The heads turned back to Yusuf, who responded, "There were certain conditions attached to acceptance of the funds. First, there was the issuance of preferred stock for ten percent of the value; that's two million. The stock can be redeemed upon return of the funds, but there is a ten percent penalty attached; that's two hundred thousand. There were warrants issued for another ten thousand shares of common stock at book value that will have to be bought back at market price. That could cost the bank another four hundred thousand. That's six hundred thousand to start, and we haven't considered the interest that will accumulate while this transaction is finalized, since the Federal Home Loan Bank won't allow you to put the money in your interest-bearing treasury account once the return procedure is affirmed, so the loan will continue to accumulate interest expense. Just some facts I am sure your board is already aware of but needed to be emphasized." Yusuf smiled, sitting straight with his hands folded.

The heads turned back to J.R., who was fuming, breathing hard, and calculating his next move. "This d-d-deal was n-n-never a-approved. N-no d-deal. There w-w-was n-no deal." J.R. stood and leaned on the table, "This b-b-board n-never a-approved th-the m-money. N-no deal."

This time, heads didn't turn because everyone was so shocked by J.R.'s stuttering.

Yusuf continued with a broad smile, "Where's Howie Mandel when you really need him?" Much to Yusuf's relief, Father Tom snickered at the remark but immediately sank back into his seat under J.R.'s severe stare. "Anyway, to a healthy bank like this, six hundred thousand-plus probably won't do much damage. You might have to skip a dividend or two until the profit margin goes back up, but your stock holders will understand."

Fred Chin Lee said, "Is that right, J.R.? No more dividends? That could hurt. I mean, it could hurt the reputation of the bank."

"Now," Yusuf began, feeling the ball rolling in his favor, "say you don't return the funds. Say you don't do anything and accept the terms of the deal and hit the deal button." He glanced at Father Tom, who allowed a faint smile to crack his face.

"By my calculations, that money will easily earn your bank and stockholders about five hundred thousand in interest over the next twelve months. Let's say you decide to participate the way the program was intended, by investing in your community, loaning the money for worthy projects and utilizing inter-bank lending. You will be helping your community and the entire economy. Then this board and the stockholders of this bank can stand tall, might even get some good press."

The heads turned back to J.R., and Father Tom cleared his throat and said, "Maybe we could put the wing on the chapel we have been talking about for twenty years."

Bellows, unusually sober said, "I heard today a fellow is in town talking about building an amusement park. Coasters and the whole works—could be the largest in the state when he's through. That's confidential, by the way. I only mention it because we are in this private meeting, but the other commissioners and I are arranging to, well, you know, get more information. That's all I can say." He held up his hands, shaking them, suggesting he did not want to take questions and continued. "But he might need financing, and I could be instrumental in leading him to our bank."

"Wait, wait," J.R. said with exasperation. "Don't you understand? This isn't free money. If the church couldn't afford to expand for the past twenty years, what's changed? There are all kinds of strings attached to this money; it's the government." J.R. raised his hand and pointed a long finger at Yusuf. "And it's sitting right there."

Sid Johnson the contractor had been quiet up to this point, but Bellows had inspired his participation. "J.R., if Ralph's information is right, some big company wants to build a big amusement park. Think about the jobs, construction jobs. They'll need financing. Why can't we think about this for a while?"

"Sid, when was the last time Ralph had any information that was accurate? He probably heard it in one of the bars." J.R. turned to Ralph and continued. "Okay, Ralph, who's this big money man? Got any idea?"

Ralph made a gruff noise, crossed his arms on his distended stomach and said, "I told you; it's confidential."

J.R. turned back to Sid. "There. Satisfied? It's confidential because there is no big money man. Who in his right mind would come to Hinkley and build Disneyland, or Hinkleyland or whatever? We don't even have a paved airport, and you think someone is going to spend millions building an amusement park?"

Yusuf, sensing the dissention, said, "J.R., maybe Sid is right. Why don't you all postpone this decision and think about it for a while. Maybe some of the unknowns will become clearer, and everyone will be able to come to a consensus."

"This is not right," J.R. complained as his influence over the group dwindled and he slumped back in his chair. "You can't just come in here and tell us what to do. We have a-a-a vote."

Father Tom held up his hand, as if he was requesting to use the restroom. "I move we adjourn and give this some consideration."

J.R. went erect again and said with authority, "You what? Y-y-you can't move a-a-anything. I-I-I make th-the motions a-and I'm n-not moving a-anything."

Yusuf interrupted. "I understand you have dinner immediately after the meeting. Everyone ready to order?"

Roger Witherspoon

Chapter 10

The Hinkley County commissioner's office phone was ringing off the hook with inquiries about the amusement park. *Where was it going to be built? When would construction start? Where could people apply for a job?* The most asked question: *Who is the big-money man who will be spearheading the project?*

Roger Witherspoon's name was prominent in every conversation. He was presumed to be the investor's local legal representative and spokesperson.

The phone in Witherspoon and Witherspoon's office rang, and Red Redderson, editor of the *Hinkley Messenger*, asked to talk to Roger Witherspoon.

"What do you mean 'he's unavailable'?"

"Mr. Witherspoon is in conference right now."

"With who?" Redderson pressed.

"I can't give out that information."

FIRST STATE BANK and (dis)TRUST of Hinkley County

"Come on, Amanda. Give up the 'I'm an important legal secretary' crap. Is he talking to the amusement park guy?"

Amanda let a big sigh fill the airwaves and let Redderson listen to the static for a few seconds. "Remember that time I called you about running the free ad for the Hinkley County Floppy-Eared Rabbit Club, Mr. 'I'm an important newspaper guy' Redderson? Screw you and your newspaper." She hung up.

Roger Witherspoon stepped out of his office. "Who was that?"

"Nobody important," Amanda responded.

"Look, if anyone calls about this amusement park thing, come get me over at Ralphy's; this is real important."

"Sure, whatever you say." Amanda picked up her pencil and went back to working her crossword puzzle.

"Did you Google that guy's name?"

"Yeah, I did, but this computer is so old and the nine-ninety-five dial-up you use in this office is so slow it might be tomorrow before we get any info. Probably be better off going to the library and using their free service," Amanda said sarcastically.

Witherspoon ignored her comments and pulled his suit coat from the coat rack. "Keep trying. It's something like Bitter Quizno or Better Quincy, or something like that. Keep trying; I need to talk to him."

HINKLEY MESSENGER, July 14, 2009
Byline: Red Redderson, Editor
AMUSEMENT PARK PLAN CONFIRMED

A county official who asked to remain anonymous confirmed today that plans are progressing for a major project in Hinkley County. Although the location and the developer's name have not been announced, the official reported that there have been informal negotiations regarding local and state incentives to assist in the planned project. Although details are unconfirmed by the developer, the planned project includes a hotel convention center and amusement park.

The Illinois Department of Economic Development declined to comment on the project, but said their representatives are intimately involved in all phases of economic development in Hinkley County. They also said they estimate a project of this magnitude would create at least 250 new jobs and have an approximate monetary impact of twenty million dollars annually on the local economy. An attempt to contact the developer's local legal representative was unsuccessful.

Harold Hanover, president of the Hinkley County Chamber of Commerce, said, "This is marvelous news; it's what we have been hoping for—a major job-producing project that could impact the entire region. This could be the start of a new era for the county. We could become a tourist destination for the entire state, even the entire mid-west. Our staff has been in contact with Seven Flags and several other amusement park developers inquiring about the project. The news is positive, that's all I can say."

Chet Sadinski, chairman of the Board of County Commissioners would not comment other than to say he had not talked personally to the developer. County Commissioner Ralph Bellows said, "The developer has requested the location and size of the project be kept confidential until a formal announcement can be made. We don't want any speculators making land grabs in anticipation of a quick buck." When asked what Commissioner Bellows meant by 'we', and if he was an investor, he declined comment.

BitterQuince

Chapter 11

J.R. walked into the bank and as usual, ignored everyone, making a direct route to his office. As he passed Sally, he said, "In my office." Sally did not look up, although she had nothing on her desk to look at.

J.R. slammed his door while Sally checked her nails, pulled her little mirror out and touched up her lipstick. She eventually stood and shook out her hair before slowly turning, and without knocking, entered J.R.'s office.

J.R. sat behind his desk reading the *Hinkley Messenger* and said, "Took you long enough." He swiveled his chair, reading the paper with his back to her. "It is unbelievable to me how gullible the people of this town can be. Amusement park," he chuckled. "Have you seen Ernest Eisley? Did he come to work today?"

"I don't keep track of Pucker, although lately it appears someone should. Yeah, he's here, sittin' over there, staring at me. Why don't you just fire him? God, he's some kind of pervert, isn't he? That should be reason enough to fire him."

"Sally, don't you ever think before you talk?" J.R. swiveled to face her. He saw the lip starting to protrude. "Oh, quit that. Look, he knows too much. I still haven't figured out where he came up with the idea to follow us to the Best Western, but we need to find out. That's what I want you to do."

"Me? You want me to do what?"

"It should be easy. Just get close to him. You know, be friendly, and ask him what's going on," J.R. said, resuming his perusal of the paper.

"Are you nuts? I'm not getting within thirty feet of that pervert. You want to know what's going on, call him into this office, and threaten to shoot him. That's easy enough. Just pull out a big handgun and point it at his head and say, 'Okay, Pucker, what the fuck's going on?'"

J.R. looked up from his paper. "Don't use that kind of language in this office."

"Then don't ask me to do stupid things." Sally crossed her arms.

"Look, all I'm asking is to maybe accidently, on purpose, meet him walking home or something, make some conversation, and find out what he wants. If it's money, I may have to get tough. If it's, I don't' know, like a promotion or something, I will have to handle it."

J.R. went back to his paper.

Sally got up and headed for the door.

J.R. threw his last comment at her back. "Just let me know what you find out."

Sally opened the door and prepared to give it a slam that the whole bank would recognize, but then saw Bit sitting next to her desk, smiling and holding his Stetson in his lap. She lightly closed the door, adjusted her dress, and walked out to her desk.

Bit followed her with his eyes and said, "How you doin' today, Miss?"

Sally beamed. This was the most handsome man she had seen in Hinkley since John Edwards made a stop during the last election campaign. One of her most precious possessions was the picture of John Edwards with his arm around her as he exited the

Hinkley high school auditorium after his speech. He offered her the chance to ride in the bus with him to their next stop in Peoria, but at the last second, one of his assistants suggested it might not be a good idea since Mrs. Edwards was en route, as well. He waved to her as the bus pulled out of the parking lot. That was the point in her life that she realized goals could never be set too high.

"Can I help you, Mr.—" She left the question linger, waiting for a name.

"Bitter Quince, but my friends—and I hope that includes you—call me Bit."

Sally gave a big smile and said, "Well, Bit, my name's Sally. What can I do for you?"

"Well, Sally, we can start with getting me acquainted with the president of this bank. I think his name is Roberts. And if that works out, maybe you'll have lunch with me. Whaddaya think? Is it a deal?" Bit uncrossed his legs and started to get up.

"I think that might work. Just sit still for a minute." Sally got up and whirled for J.R.'s door. Opening the door and sticking her head in, she said, "J.R., there's someone here you have to talk to. I'll send him in."

Before J.R. could even look up, she opened the door all the way and stepped back. She turned to Bit and almost curtsied as she waved her hand, inviting him to enter.

J.R. rumbled, "Wait a minute. What? Who is... I don't want to see anyone."

Bit walked through the door and winked at Sally as he passed. "How y'all doin' today? My name is Bitter Quince, but my friends call me Bit." Bit closed the door behind him.

J.R. sat with his hands still on his computer, looking at Bit. "Who are you? I don't want to see anyone right now, so leave." J.R. started pushing buttons on his intercom. "Sally, what's going on? Get this guy out of here."

Bit sat down and adjusted his sport coat, getting relaxed. "No need to get excited, Mr. Roberts. I'm just here to talk banking business. That's what you do, right?"

FIRST STATE BANK and (dis)TRUST of Hinkley County

"What's your name again? Wait, I don't need to know your name because I don't want to talk to you."

"This the way you treat all your new customers? Surprised you have any. As I said, my name's Bitter Quince, but my friends call me Bit. So far, you probably ought to call me Mr. Quince, but that could easily change. See, Mr. Roberts, I'm thinkin' about doin' some business in your town, maybe build a motel—might even have one of those fancy water slide deals. You know what I mean?"

J.R. looked up, a wry smile on his face. "So you're the amusement park guy everyone's talking about."

"I don't reckon I ever said anything about an amusement park, but what the hell—you never know where things might lead. Here's the deal Mis— Mind if we drop the formalities? My name's Bit, what's yours?"

J.R. hesitated for a second and then slowly, as if it hurt him to say it, "J.R.; J.R. Roberts."

"Okay, J.R.; that's better. Where I come from, all that mister and missus stuff is just for the older folks, to show respect. Anyway, as I started to say, I've been lookin' for a small community that's been neglected. When I say neglected, I mean one that hasn't had all the big development already. Don't mean it isn't going to happen, but I want to be ahead of it. So, I was thinkin' about maybe putting up a motel, somewhere close to the four-lane, but still part of the town. Have a swimmin' pool, maybe a fancy restaurant, something for the locals to enjoy for a night or maybe a weekend. Whaddaya think?"

J.R. thought for a minute before saying, "And you've done this before?"

Bit smiled, ran his hand through his thick, sun-bleached hair, and said, "I've done a few things, mostly in oil towns. That's where I got started—in the oil business. My daddy ran a mobile rig in northern Oklahoma. We're originally from Kansas, but the family made its way to Oklahoma when oil got big. My daddy did real well for a few years, but then things got tough, and he got old—wore out, mostly. Anyway, I kinda struck out on my own. Had a grub stake from selling daddy's rig and bought some mineral rights in the Jackson Flats area of western Oklahoma, thinkin' I would wildcat a little, and wouldn't you know it? Old Texaco decided they wanted those rights more than me because it was right in the middle of a big play they were making. I started looking at some other areas where the big boys were investing and made a few more deals, and before I knew it, I'm like Jed Clampet. I'm movin' to Beverly Hills, swimmin' pools and movie stars.

"Anyway, I decided to get out of the oil business and start working in real estate—a lot cleaner, and the girls are a lot better lookin'. I look for small towns that need a little jab in the rear to get them goin'. Looks to me like this town might need a little more than a jab, but it has potential." Bit sat back, waited for J.R. to absorb his commentary, and then continued, "If I follow my routine, I'm lookin' at about eight mil, at least to start. That'll get you about fifty rooms under a good flag like Fairfield or Hampton, depending on the cost of the real estate."

"So why are you talking to me? I don't sell real estate," J.R. said curtly.

Bit made a motion with his head as if he was looking at the surroundings. "This is a bank, isn't it? And last time I checked, most banks make loans."

"Doesn't sound like you need a loan; sounds more like you need a place to keep your money. You want to make a deposit? We can handle that."

Bit smiled and leaned forward. "Man, you are a tough one, aren't you? I bet this bank makes plenty of money, and I bet you know the name of every customer that's over three days late on a payment. No matter—you've told me enough without saying anything. You're the kinda fellow I want on my team. It shouldn't take long to get everything lined up, and then I'll be back to talk about financing. I understand y'all are getting a big chunk of the free government money, so it shouldn't be too difficult for me to get a slice of that pie."

J.R. stood up as if he was catapulted from an ejection chair. "Who told you that? I want to know who told you that. Was it Ralph Bellows, the county commissioner?"

FIRST STATE BANK and (dis)TRUST of Hinkley County

"Whoa, calm down there, partner; you're gonna pop a blood vessel. Don't worry about where I get my information; it's secure." Bit stood, adjusted his jacket, and reached across the desk to shake. "Nice meetin' you, J.R.; I think we are gonna get along just fine. Next time I come in, hope you got that checkbook ready."

Bit strolled out of the office and up to Sally's desk. He looked at his watch and said, "You ready for lunch, darlin'? I heard this place called Ralphy's just down the street makes some Texas red chili that'll make your throat burn. Ain't nothin' better than hot chili and cold beer."

Sally Butterbetter

Chapter 12

Bit led Sally through the door into Ralphy's, and the usual lunch commotion went silent as every head turned to look at the tall, tan, well dressed man. Bit just smiled and said, "How y'all doin'?"

The lunch crowd resumed their conversations, and Bit led Sally to an empty booth. As they sat down, Roger Witherspoon slithered off his bar stool, walked over, and rested his arm on the booth divider, anticipating an invitation to sit down, but none was offered.

"Hey, Bit," said Roger. "Been looking all over for you. You really have the town talking, asking a lot of questions. Mind if I sit down for a minute? Like to talk to you, if I can."

Bit removed his hat and rested it on the seat next to him. "This ain't a very good time to be askin' me questions, uh—" Bit searched for a name.

Sally spoke in a less than interested tone. "Witherspoon. It's Roger Witherspoon. He's some kind of attorney, I guess."

"Well, Roger," Bit said, "you're making me choose between talkin' to you or this here lovely lady, and buddy, you don't stand a chance. Why don't you mosey back over to the bar, and the next time I'm around, I promise I'll talk to you."

"Yeah, but Bit, people need to know about all this amusement park stuff, and I thought, well—you know—I could be your spokesman." Witherspoon leaned over the table, a little too close for Sally, and she scooted in the opposite direction.

Bit slid out of the booth, and in a single motion grabbed Roger by the back of his shirt, lifting him like he was a wooden ventriloquist's doll, and guided him across the room to the bar. "Roger, I asked nice the first time, but you don't seem to listen. I always heard that's one of the first things they teach you in law school—how to listen. Now you stay over here, and we'll stay over there, and everyone will be happy and enjoy their lunch, understand?"

Ralphy came briskly down the bar. "What's going on here?"

Bit looked at Roger and said, "No problem—is there, Roger?"

Roger looked up at Ralphy, his face gaunt with fear. "No problem, no problem at all."

Bit returned to his booth and slid in, smiling. "Now then, aren't you just cute as a newborn lamb? So, Sally, I guess I never asked your last name."

Sally saw the opportunity to use her 'innocent as a preacher's daughter' card and said, "Butterbetter. My father's the pastor of the Body of Christ on the Cross Baptist Church." She fluttered her eyelashes as she looked up from her folded hands.

Bit had trouble withholding his laughter. He already had a complete dossier on J.R. Roberts, and Sally was a prominent figure in the biography. "So, you grew up here and graduated from high school here as well?"

"For the most part. We moved here when I was about ten. Preachers move around a lot, and I have been here ever since. I've worked at the bank for five years and been Mr. Roberts' personal assistant for the past four years."

"Tough guy to work for, I bet," Bit said, leaning back and resting his arms over the divider. "He seemed a little tense this morning, as if he'd just heard his car was getting repossessed."

"Oh, he was just upset about one of the employees. Found out he's a pervert—likes to show his Johnson." Sally thought better of her wording, since she was still trying to play the innocence card and retracted. "Likes to expose himself, I guess. I mean, I've never seen it. He's never done it to me. I mean, you know, pulled it out—whatever." Sally sighed in relief when she finally shut her mouth.

"And he works at the bank, huh? He do that in the bank—show himself?"

"No, last time I guess was at a motel—peeking in windows." Sally couldn't help but stare at those blue eyes and that boyish face, complete with dimples that deepened every time Bit smiled, which was a lot. "Bit, that's a funny name. What is it, Bitter or Better? Is that short for something?"

"Just short for humorous. My daddy had a sense of humor that most didn't understand. You know what a quince is? It's a fruit, grows in the wild, and in some places, they cultivate it. It's kind of a cross between a crabapple and a pear. If you pick it at just the right time, it's not bad to cook with, but otherwise, it's real bitter. Get it? Bitter Quince. We used to have a quince tree on our ranch in Kansas. I always thought somewhere along the line, maybe my daddy's daddy had to change his name due to some indiscretion the family don't talk about, and looked at that tree and said, 'Quince sounds like a good last name.'"

Sally felt the thump, thump, thump of her heartbeat, the blush of heat on her face, and the warmth of lust in her loins. She took a deep breath to calm herself.

"You okay? Here I am talkin' like a high school kid and you're probably hungry. Want to try some of that chili?" Bit threw up his hand to get the attention of the sole waitress that was running around the room.

Sally wanted to grab his hand and say, "No food, no food," but instead she tried to reengage the conversation. "I take it you're not married. At least, you don't wear a ring."

FIRST STATE BANK and (dis)TRUST of Hinkley County

"Naw, travel too much to make anyone feel, you know, wanted—the way women need to feel. Now, that's not to say I haven't broken a few hearts, and there's still a couple that like to think I'll get off the bronc someday and settle for a saddle mare, but it ain't happened yet. I recon they'll keep waitin'."

Jesse the waitress passed their booth and caught a glimpse of Bit, which made her put on her brakes like she was making a NASCAR pit stop.

"How we doin' today?" Bit said, smiling.

"Just fine, babe, how 'bout you?" Jesse smiled and then looked at Sally, a known adversary when it came to single men in town and the smile stiffened. "Get you two anything to drink?"

"I'll have one of those cold long necks. What about you, Sally?" Bit asked.

"I'll have a raspberry wine cooler," Sally replied, never taking her eyes off Bit.

"I'll have to see some ID," Jesse said, crooking her arm on her waist. Jesse had gone to high school with Sally. She knew exactly how old Sally was.

Sally slowly turned and looked at Jesse. "Piss off, Jesse. Just get my drink."

Bit leaned back in the booth and put his arms up on the divider seeming to enjoy the confrontation.

"You know the rules, Sally; I have to see an ID. This gentleman—what did you say your name is?"

"Bitter. Bitter Quince, but my friends just call me Bit."

"Bit here may work for the state, and the law says if I think someone looks a little young and immature," she emphasized the last word, "I need to see some ID. You understand, don't you, Bit?" Jesse gave Bit a big smile.

Sally started to say something that Bit knew wasn't going to be very lady-like so he interrupted. "Jesse, Sally here didn't bring her confidentials with her. Now, we both know she's old enough to drink in this state, so I'd really appreciate it if you would make an exception this one time, just for me. I'll make it up to you, darlin,' I promise."

Jesse gave Sally a smirk and then leaned over, putting her hand on the table, turning away from Sally and smiled at Bit. "You got a way don't you? Can make a woman do about anything you want. I'll be back with your drinks." She turned and headed for the bar.

Bit rested his elbows on the table. "I don't think she cares for you much. Not unusual when they know you're the prettiest girl in the place."

Thump, thump, thump. Sally's mouth was dry, and everything else was wet.

"You ever notice anything unusual at the bank? I mean, like unusual people coming or going, or your boss doing anything that seems, you know, out of the ordinary?" Bit asked off the top of his head.

The question caught Sally off-guard—the conversation had been so personal up to this point, and she had been swept so far off her feet she felt like she was floating above the booth. "Uh, I'm not sure what you mean. Why do you want to know about him? He's just my boss."

"Well, I'm thinking about doing some business with him, the bank, and it's important that everything is on the up and up. You know, with all this stuff in the news about banks and the executives walking away with all the money, I'm just bein' careful." Bit glanced at the bar and saw Jesse staring at him and smiling as she waited for the drinks.

"I've never seen anyone unusual, other than the big black guy that was in about a week or two ago. I think he was from the government or something." Sally's euphoria eroded, and she slumped back in the booth.

"Oh, yeah? He talk to you any? Say what he wanted or anything?"

Jesse arrived with the drinks and placed Sally's wine cooler in front of her without a glass. She gave Bit a frosted mug and said smoothly, "Want me to pour it for you, babe?"

"No, thanks." Bit slid the frosted glass across the table to Sally as Jesse whirled and walked away. "The big guy, did you catch his name?"

FIRST STATE BANK and (dis)TRUST of Hinkley County

Sally studied Bit's expression and said, "It was some African name. I really don't remember. Why, is that important?" Sally crossed her arms with some attitude.

"Don't you worry your pretty little head. It's not important. Just trying to get a feel for the way things are done around here. See, every town has its own personality. Some towns, the politicians run everything; others, it's the bankers; and still others, you can't find anyone that knows what's goin' on. I get the feelin' your boss is pretty much the go-to guy around here. You hungry? I think I need some of that chili, assuming you don't need an ID to eat in this joint."

The humor made Sally relax. "The burgers aren't too bad, either." Sally hesitated and then continued, "Bit, I know we just met, but I need some advice, or at least a second opinion."

"This ain't some girlie thing, is it? I mean, doctorin' ain't somethin' I have much experience in, although I have whelped a few lambs in my day. I suppose that's pretty close."

"Oh, God, no." Sally erupted in laughter. "You are something, Bitter Quince. This isn't about me. I mean, well, you know what I mean; it's about something my boss asked me to do."

Jesse stopped at the table. "Ready to order, or are you two just going to drink?"

Bit looked at Sally, giving her a chance to speak, and then said, "I'll have some of that chili and another beer. What do you think, Sally?"

Jesse tapped her pencil on her order pad impatiently. Sally scowled up at Jesse and said, "I'll just drink."

Sally adjusted herself in the seat and began again. "Remember what I said about Pucker? That's the pervert in the bank. Well J.R.—Mr. Roberts—wants me to kind of spy on him. Well, really not spy, but get close enough to find out what he's doing or what he wants."

"You already said y'all know what he's doing. What's there to find out?"

Sally sighed in exasperation. "Well, it's a little more complicated than that. See, he may have seen J—Mr. Roberts doing something…actually we… He thinks Pucker may have followed him. So, he wants me to meet with Pucker and, you know, try to get him to tell me what he's up to."

"This Pucker—that what you call him? You think he's dangerous?"

"Dangerous? Pucker? No way. He's perverted. You know, he lives with his mother and wears matching clothes and stupid looking glasses. He looks a little like that guy—what's his name? Holly, from way back."

"Buddy Holly, the big bopper?"

Just as Bit finished his question, Jesse brought his chili and said, "The big bopper? You like Buddy Holly? He's one of my favorites—played with the Crickets. We have some of that on the jukebox. Stick around until this crowd thins, and I'll dance you around these tables like you never been danced before."

Sally looked up and said, "I think Ralphy wants you at the bar."

Jesse instinctively turned to look at the bar and then, realizing she was being dismissed, gave Sally a hard look and stomped off.

"See how this town is?" Sally said with a disgusted look on her face. "You can't even have lunch without someone getting in your face."

"Okay," Bit continued, some concern in his voice, "this Pucker—he young, old, what?"

Sally, sensing she was garnering a little sympathy, played it hard. "He's about my age, graduated about the same time, but he didn't have any friends, and never did anything in school except stand around in the corner and stare. I mean, if you saw him, you would understand what I'm talking about. He's one of those guys that walk around with a sign on his back that says 'punch me'."

"Sounds pretty sad, to tell you the truth. How do you know I wasn't one of those guys?" Bit said as he nursed his chili.

Sally laughed and said sarcastically, "Yeah, sure. You've got geek written all over you."

"You think if you don't do what J.R. asks he'll fire you?"

"Are you kidding? I've got so much on him he—" Sally hesitated and then said, "No, he won't fire me."

"So why even think about talkin' to this Pucker?"

Sally contemplated for a few seconds. "I suppose I owe it to J.R. He's been pretty good to me."

Bit looked up from his chili and their eyes locked. Sally looked away, but the guilt couldn't be hidden. Bit said, "Well, a girl's got to do what a girl's got to do."

"That's it? That's the best advice you can give?" Sally said harshly, but then smiled. "I guess it was stupid of me to bring it up."

Bit took the last bite of the chili and chased it with the last swallow of beer. "Not at all. I'm glad you did. Here's what I suggest—we'll do a little 'I rub your back, you rub my back.'"

Sally smiled brightly and said, "Now you're talking." She put her elbows on the table and folded both hands under her chin, her emerald eyes wide in anticipation of the next sentence.

"I don't mean literally. Not yet, anyway." Bit smiled back. "I'll help you with the Pucker thing if you help me with some issues at the bank—nothing too difficult for you—and I'll just help get the info from Pucker and keep an eye out so he doesn't get too frisky."

"Where we going to do this planning?" Thump, thump, thump. Sally's heat meter was peaking again.

"Man, you are something. I'll have to think about that one. But for right now, let's just keep this between the two of us. You tell J.R. that you are gonna go along, help him stiff Pucker for information. I need you to let me know if there is any communication between the guy you mentioned and J.R. If he shows up, you call me. I'm gonna give you my cell, but you have to guard the number with your life. And don't call me from the bank. You have your own cell phone?"

"Sure," Sally said, pulling the phone from some hidden pocket. "Doesn't everyone? Anyway, why are you so interested in the government guy?"

"Now, see, that's where we have to be discreet about all this, and that's why I think you can do this. You've been pretty discreet about your business with J.R., so I figure you can keep my business quiet as well."

"What business with J.R.?" Sally crossed her arms in a defensive gesture.

"It ain't too tough to figure out what's goin' on, Sally. Don't worry, I'm not gonna ruin anything. You're an adult, no matter what that waitress says." Bit gave her a big smile, but the humor didn't sit well with Sally, and she just stared at him. "You know, you have some of the most beautiful eyes, and when you get upset, they kind of glow; it's amazing."

Sally melted under the barrage of compliments. "It's not like we're in love or anything. Like I said, he's been good to me in a lot of ways."

"Can't beat that with a stick," Bit said, reaching in his pocket and pulling out the rubber band entwined wad of bills. "Let's see." He fished through the hundreds looking for a smaller bill. "Here we go." He threw a twenty down on the table. "Ready to go back to work?"

Sally's eyes moved from the wad of money to Bit's smiling face, and her amazement turned to childish euphoria. "I need your cell number, just in case, you know, the big guy shows up again, and where did you say you are staying?"

Edna Eisley

Chapter 13

Tuesday nights were always special in the Eisley household. The World Wrestling Association had their weekly match at eight o'clock, and Pucker and his mother gathered in front of the Sony and rooted for their favorite pro wrestler.

In advance of the eventful evening, Pucker always left the bank, walked the half-mile down Main Street to the Hinkley Family Bowling Center, bought an extra-large bag of popcorn and a family pack of fried chicken (considered the best in the county), and made his way home, arriving in time to make a cursory inspection of the flower beds surrounding their small house, pulling weeds and pruning petunias.

Pucker walked out of the bowling alley, the brown paper grocery sack containing fried chicken and popcorn in hand, and briskly walked across the parking lot toward Main Street. Sally, who was sitting in her convertible waiting for him to exit, put the car in gear and tore across the parking lot, screeching to a halt just as he reached the sidewalk. The sound of the squealing tires almost caused him to lose grip of the bag.

"Pucker, need a ride?" Sally called from the driver's seat.

Pucker stood, mouth open, not comprehending the question. He looked around for another bystander, since Sally had never so much as looked at him before, let alone offered him a ride.

"Earth to Pucker. Put your antenna up. I'm talking to you." Sally opened her door, showing her legs, her skirt pulled up far enough to be provocative. "I asked if you want a ride. You going home? Roll a couple games after work? Speak up, Pucker; I'm getting tired of talking to myself."

"I-I... Well, Miss Butterbetter, this is a surprise. You want me, right now, to get in with you?" Pucker took a half step closer to the car.

Sally saw the grease from the paper bag soaking through onto Pucker's white shirt. She leaned her head on the steering wheel. "Jesus, I can't believe I'm doing this." Louder, looking up, "You want a ride or not? God, Pucker, you're getting that greasy stuff all over your shirt. Don't get any of that on my car." Sally reached over her seat, got a folded towel from the back seat, and then opened the passenger door from the inside. "Here, wipe that stuff off and get in here."

Pucker slowly, apprehensively, walked around the car, approaching the passenger door, then stopped and said slowly, "You want me to sit in the back?"

"You've got about two seconds to get your butt in this car, or I'm leaving. Am I getting through to you? Jesus, Pucker, do you act this stupid in the teller window?"

He started to get in, then decided he better take the towel first and started to put the sack on the ground, then realized that was probably a bad idea, so he adjusted his body to rest the bag on his leg while he reached for the towel. Once he had accomplished that, he tried to unwrap the towel and cover the seat, still trying to balance the bag on his hitched leg, looking a little like a poorly choreographed circus act.

Sally slapped herself in the forehead, cursed, got out of the car, came around to the passenger door, and daintily took the sack out of Pucker's arms, holding it away from her blouse and skirt while he finished fitting the towel on the seat. Pucker then looked back at Sally, waiting for permission to enter the car.

Sally pushed the sack back in his arms. "Get in, Pucker. My God, are you always like this?"

While Pucker slowly crawled into the passenger seat, making sure he didn't touch anything with the greasy sack, Sally looked across the parking lot at the Escalade sitting near the bowling alley building. She threw up her hands in exasperation, stomped around the car, and got in. She put the car in gear and blew out of the parking lot toward the outskirts of town, away from Pucker's house.

Pucker sat quietly looking straight ahead, the grease percolating through the sack onto his lap. Sally watched each car as it passed, hoping not to recognize anyone. Pucker still did not say anything, which seemed strange to Sally. She at least thought he would suggest she had taken an errant turn if she intended to take him home.

The Escalade trailed behind, Bit having no difficulty keeping them in view with the light traffic.

Pucker stared straight ahead as Sally entered the four-lane that led to Cougar Falls, her intended destination a little-used rest stop about a half-mile down the road.

Rolling to a stop in the rest area, Sally jammed the car into park as Pucker said, "That's okay; I don't need to use the restroom. I went at the bowling alley."

"Good for you," Sally said, staring straight ahead, looking at the same nothingness Pucker seemed to be fixated on. She turned and started to say something, but noticed the growing grease stain on Pucker's pants. "Pucker, for God's sake, you're like a little kid. Give me that sack; I'll put it in the trunk." Sally pushed the button for the trunk lid and took the sack from Pucker, holding it well away from her clothing. She got out and put the sack in the trunk. As she closed the lid, the Escalade slowly drove by them and parked at the other end of the lot.

Sally got back in the car. Pucker was still staring straight ahead, his hands folded on his greasy lap. Sally began the interrogation tactfully. "You bowl often?"

"I don't care to bowl."

"Okay, so what do you do at the bowling alley? Just hang out in the restroom?" Sally felt bad as soon as she finished the comment. Pucker's stare did not change, but she saw a slight twitch in his eye. "Sorry, I didn't mean that. Just a joke. What's in the bag?"

"Dinner. My mother likes their chicken. Can I go home now?"

This was more difficult than Sally imagined. She thought she would just confront him with some mean-spirited questions, kind of the way TV prosecutors do, and Pucker would just break down and spill the beans. As it turned out, she was starting to feel sorry for him, the poor schmuck. "I understand you had a problem at the Best Western. What was that all about?"

"It was just a mistake. Miss Butterbetter, I would like to go home now."

"Call me Sally. What kind of mistake? You mean you made a mistake, or the police made a mistake?"

"It was all a mistake. I know I am probably going to be fired and I understand; you can tell Mr. Roberts that. He's a great man and I embarrassed him; it was just a mistake." Pucker's eye twitched twice this time.

Sally saw an opportunity to gain his confidence and maybe some information. "Well, I might be able to help—I mean with the getting fired part. Mr. Roberts does listen to me, not all the time, but I could talk to him."

Pucker looked at her for the first time. "Why would you do that?"

That's a good question, Sally thought. "Well, you are in the Teller's Hall of Fame, and if it was a mistake following Mr. Roberts to the Best Western, maybe he will change his mind."

"I didn't follow him. Why would I follow him?" Pucker's intense stare did not leave Sally.

"Uh, that's a good question." Sally for the first time was glad Bit was within screaming distance. "It's just a little strange, you being right there, looking in his window."

"It seemed a little strange that you were right there, looking out of his window," Pucker responded without delay.

Sally tried to evade the implication. "I still don't understand, Pucker. Why were you there? There had to be some reason you were looking in his window. The policeman said that's what he saw you do, along with other things we really don't need to go into."

Pucker sighed, turned, and stared straight ahead again. "I thought he was being kidnapped. I thought someone was robbing the bank."

"You're kidding, right?"

"See, there's no use discussing this. Will you please take me home?" This time, Pucker crossed his arms with a little attitude.

"Okay, sorry. Tell me the rest of the story. Why would you think we, I mean he was being kidnapped?"

Pucker sat quietly for a few seconds, sighed again, and started from the top, from him standing at the bus stop, not leaving out any details, telling her about the movie and including the part where he soiled himself and why his zipper was down. When he finished, he looked at Sally, who was biting her lip to keep from laughing.

"Damn, Pucker, you're about the unluckiest thing I've ever met." She couldn't help but think, *why am I feeling sorry for this guy? He's a complete nerd.* She almost wanted to reach over and give him a hug just to comfort him after hearing his story. It was so ridiculous; it had to be true. *I have the power to do something about this.* "Okay, Pucker—Ernest—we are going to fix this with J... Mr. Roberts. You aren't going to lose your job; you might even get a raise. After all, you were just trying to save the bank."

Sally started the car, and as they drove out of the rest area, she gave the thumbs up sign to Bit.

FIRST STATE BANK and (dis)TRUST of Hinkley County

Sally stopped the car in front of Pucker's house, got out, and retrieved the bag from the trunk. "Just go to work tomorrow as usual, and don't worry about J.R. And don't sit over there at your teller station and look up my dress, okay? If you want to talk to me, just come over to my desk. I'll talk, as long as you don't act like some kind of goofball."

As Pucker walked up the steps to the porch, Edna Eisley came crashing out of the front door, and Sally heard, "Who was that woman? Was that Sally Butterbetter? Where have you been? Ernest Eisley, don't you lie to me."

Sally Butterbetter

CHAPTER 14

J.R. poured over binders of continuous feed computer paper delivered to his desk by John White. So far, the T.A.R.P. funds had generated over twenty thousand dollars of interest income, and they hadn't loaned a penny, merely bought short-term treasuries, moved funds to other institutions as short-term loan transfers, and carried the balance as surplus. Since the last board meeting, he had not contacted any board member and felt sure they were too intimidated to call him.

His intercom buzzed, and he picked up the receiver and gruffly answered, "Who is it?"

"It's the Yusuf guy—Olagawaga or something." Sally hung up the intercom and immediately walked to J.R.'s office and entered.

J.R. answered the phone just as Sally entered. "This is Jerome Roberts." J.R. put his hand over the phone and said to Sally, "What do you want? I'm on the phone." Then, "Okay, things are fine here."

Sally whispered, "I need to talk to you about Pucker." That topic was the only thing that would interest J.R. enough to allow her to stay in the office.

J.R. pointed to the chair, signaling her to sit down, and swiveled in his chair, turning his back to her and continuing his conversation. "Uh-huh, well, we still are not decided on that.   No, we haven't met again…….. I don't think I'm obligated to let you know about our meetings…………. I don't care what Buckminster said………….. Did I talk to whom?……….   Bitter what? You talking about the cowboy that's spreading all the money around town?……….. How do you know he's legitimate?………….. Well, he's talking about some kind of motel, and somebody said something about an amusement park. Uh-huh. Uh, huh. You don't really think I'm going to participate in something like that, do you?……….. I don't care what you think……………You go ahead and talk to the other board members. I make the decisions when it comes to loans.   I'm not upset………….. Well, you just have a fine day as well." J.R. slammed the phone down.

Sally got up. "Maybe we should talk later, after you calm down."

"I am calm," he roared. "What about Pecker or Pucker, and what was this e-mail about not going to Chicago this weekend? I thought that was all set. Buckminster got me tickets for Second City on Saturday night. That reminds me, I need to call that idiot, him telling Olaja whatever that…... Oh, never mind. What about Pucker, or Ernest? What did you find out?"

Sally sat back down and organized her thoughts. "Well, I talked to Pucker. He's a sly one, all right." She adjusted her blouse and tossed her hair back. "Didn't really want to give me much. I tried to be nice, you know—kind of play up to him, but I think he got suspicious. Anyway—"

"Good Lord, Sally, just tell me what he wants. I don't need to know the intricacies of his personality. We both know he's a kook, so what does he want?"

"He really didn't say. I mean, I tried to get out of him how he knew we, you were at the motel, but he just smiled—you know, that weird smile. He did say that that part about touching himself—that stuff didn't happen." Sally brushed imaginary lint off her blouse.

"So, what you are telling me is that you really didn't find out anything."

"This takes time, J.R. I have to gain his confidence, and then he might tell me what's going on. In the mean time, I think you should let him stay at the bank. That way, I can keep an eye on him and keep schmoozing him for information."

J.R. gave her a suspicious stare. "Last time we talked about this, you wanted me to shoot him. Now you want him to stay. I don't get it."

"Look, you asked me to do this. I don't remember volunteering for this mission. I am kissing up to a pervert, and you act as if the whole thing is my fault. And the Chicago thing—I just thought until I figure out what he knows and why he's doing this stuff, you know, maybe we should take a break. What happens if he gets upset because you fire him or get in his face, and then he goes and talks to your wife, or sends her an anonymous note or something? Ever think of that? I'm just trying to do what's best for you, J.R." Sally got up, came around the desk, and put her hand on his shoulder. "That's all I care about."

Sally stood outside the side door of the bank where the habitual smokers stood during their breaks. She dialed Bit's cell. "Hi, Bit; it's me."

"How you doin' today, darlin'?"

"He called."

"Who called?"

"The Yusuf guy, the guy you said to watch out for." Sally leaned against the wall of the building in a conspiratorial stance, even though there was no one around that could overhear her conversation.

"No kiddin'? You talk to him?"

"Of course not, Bit. Why would he talk to me? No, he talked to J.R. All I could hear was J.R.'s part, but he wasn't happy."

"Wasn't happy about what?"

Sally sighed. "Well, he's never really happy, but they talked about the board of directors, and they talked about you."

"Hot damn; that's what I wanted to hear. What'd they say?"

"Like I said, I could only hear J.R., but it was something about an amusement park. What do you have to do with an amusement park? You're not one of those guys that travels around with the rides, are you? What are they called—carnies?" Sally asked, some concern in her voice.

"Not hardly," Bit responded. "Anything else?"

Sally thought for a second. "No, that's about it, other than something about a loan, but I couldn't get much about that."

"You did just fine, hon, just fine. What say you and I have some dinner tonight? You game?"

Thump, thump, thump. Sally tried to hold back her response, not wanting to sound too excited. "I suppose, but there's not much around here—I mean good restaurants. There's the Applebee's."

"I'll tell you what. I'm stayin' over in Cougar Falls, and there's a little place called Mitsey's. You ever heard of it?"

"Well, yeah. I've seen it. Don't think I've ever been inside." Mitsey's was the classiest restaurant in the Falls. They had one hundred-dollar bottles of wine.

"You think you could find it? I don't know that it's a good idea for you to be riding around with me, not just yet."

Sally's smile was so big it stretched her cheeks. "I suppose I could meet you this time."

CHAPTER 15

The Body of Christ on the Cross Baptist Church sanctuary was filled to capacity in anticipation of the dedication ceremony for the new parsonage, built partially through the many donations to the church capital campaign that had been waged for the past four years and a sizable mortgage provided by the First State Bank and Trust Company of Hinkley County. The dedication ceremony was scheduled immediately following Pastor Butterbetter's lengthy sermon.

J.R. and Monica Roberts were seated in the V.I.P. section in the first-row pew as special guests. They had no choice but to arrive early, with no chance of an early exit. Pastor Butterbetter required his wife and family members to occupy a front pew during special services so Sally, with much dread, was seated next to Monica, even though she protested vigorously and almost knocked her mother over trying to avoid the coincidental seating arrangement when she inadvertently entered the pew. Monica, as well, found the situation distressful since she'd had an instinctual hatred for Sally from the first day she became J.R.'s personal assistant.

The V.I.P pew was filled out with Ralph Bellows and his wife, representing the political interest of the community. It was common knowledge that Ralph and his wife never missed a church or social function, regardless of the denomination, if it was followed by a free meal. In addition, several members of the Baptist hierarchy had been summoned from other parts of the state and seated conspicuously in adjoining front rows.

Edna Eisley and Pucker were life-long members of the church, and when Edna saw J.R. sitting in the front row, she pushed Pucker all the way up the center aisle to take a seat directly behind him, much to the protests of numerous influential Baptist members that had claimed the second row as their seats of preference for years.

The religious ceremony ended with a lengthy prayer by Pastor Butterbetter and a piano accompanied rendition of "A Closer Walk with Thee," sung by Margaret Butterbetter. Margaret at one time, prior to meeting and marrying Pastor Butterbetter, had been the lead singer for a country band named *Margo and the Hopalong Boys* and had been known to consume an entire case of beer during their honky-tonk performances. She awoke one Sunday morning lying naked under one of the bar's tables.

The event caused an epiphany of sorts, leading her to become a born-again Christian and join the Baptist church. Her singing prowess, along with some other physical attributes, were recognized by then-Assistant Pastor Butterbetter and she soon became Mrs. Butterbetter.

Pastor Butterbetter raised his ceremonial robe-draped arms and quieted the congregation that was enthusiastically trying to exit the sanctuary as the last note of the hymn bounced off the final wall. "We will all now, in an orderly fashion, walk around the church to the sanctuary, where we will have the official dedication, immediately followed by a luncheon in the church basement prepared by the Baptist Women of God Auxiliary."

Most of the congregation saw the opportunity to flee and made their way to the secondary exits. Pastor Butterbetter invited the V.I.P. pew to walk in front of Margaret and him, guaranteeing their participation.

Edna, pulling Pucker by his wrist, walked in step behind J.R., elbowing Ralph Bellows out of the way to gain her position. J.R. looked over his shoulder to reconnoiter Sally's position in the parade and found himself face to face with Edna. Her large, red, lipstick-coated lips parted with a big smile, while her frizzed helmet-like hair blocked his view.

"Oh, Mr. Roberts," Edna cooed. "How nice of you to attend our dedication. Ernest was just saying that y'all are Catholic, but even so, you never hesitated to loan us the money."

"What? Who? Ernest said what? What does being Catholic have to do with anything?" J.R. asked.

Pucker, sensing distaste in J.R.'s response, pulled on his mother's arm, but she just shook him off. "Ernest is so happy working at the bank." Edna peered around J.R. at Monica. "And Mrs. Roberts, that dress is just darling. It's so difficult finding anything fashionable in the plus sizes these days."

Monica's jaw dropped, but there was nothing except a gasp followed by erupting redness in her face.

Sally heard the exchange, pushed by Ralph Bellows, and interrupted, "Mrs. Eisley, how nice to see you and Ernest. Could you two give me a hand with the, uh—the the special dedication cookies?"

"What cookies?" Edna asked, a frown growing on her face. "I don't see any cookies."

Sally looked at Pucker and said, "Ernest, take your mom to the cookie room and get the cookies."

The parade continued toward the main entrance of the church, and Pucker urged his mother to get out of the line and wait for further instruction from Sally.

As Pastor Butterbetter and Margaret followed the last participants out of the door, Sally said, "Darn, someone must have already picked up the cookies. I'm sorry; we may as well go to the basement. They'll be coming back in a few minutes."

Edna's painted-on right eyebrow rose in an arched, inquisitive gesture as she stared at Sally and then slowly growled, "What's going on here?"

Edna moved closer to Sally and lowering her voice said, "First, you talk Ernest into going for a joy ride with you, and now you make up this story to get him alone in some cookie room." A smile broke across her face, revealing cracks in her crusted makeup. "Are you sweet on my Ernest?"

Sally broke into a wry smile. "Why, Mrs. Eisley, you are a quick one, aren't you? Now I know where Ernest gets his sense of humor."

The dedication was short, with exception of Pastor Butterbetter's prayer, and the entourage headed for the entrance to the church basement for lunch. J.R., relieved that the ceremony was finally over, told Monica to go to the car and he would join her shortly. He needed to talk to Ralph Bellows.

Ralph was shaking hands and slapping backs when J.R. approached. He put his hand on Ralph's shoulder and suggested they step aside for a private conversation.

J.R. got very close to Ralph, and with a tight jaw and stern whisper said, "Who did you tell about the T.A.R.P. funds? If I find out you have been talking about this all over town, not only won't you be a director of my bank, I'll make sure this is the last time you serve as commissioner. You won't even be able to run for dog catcher."

Ralph took a step back. "Whoa, there, J.R. Don't get your feathers all ruffled. I haven't talked to anyone about anything. I know when things are confidential; you don't have to worry about that."

"All right, how did the amusement park guy find out? You and the other commissioners are the only ones that have talked to him or know who he is. How did he find out?"

Ralph got a perplexed look on his face. "What amusement park guy? I haven't talked to any amusement park guy." Ralph licked his lips and looked at the group funneling into the church for lunch. "Why don't we talk about this later?"

"You said you and the other commissioners were meeting with this developer, the guy that wants to build an amusement park."

"Yeah, but I didn't say I knew who he was, did I?" Ralph's sheepish look gave credibility to his ignorance. "The only person I've talked to about any of this is the colored or African guy that was at the meeting. He called me the next day. Said he wanted to know the name of the amusement park guy. I just told him it was confidential."

"Meaning you really didn't know," J.R. said, exasperated.

"Well, yeah, I guess. Anyway, the only thing I told him was that I thought Roger Witherspoon was the guy's attorney in town and if he wanted any information he should call him." Ralph again looked at the entrance to the church. "Don't you think we ought to get in there?"

"So Olajuwon called you. What else did he say?" J.R. grasped Ralph's arm as Ralph leaned toward the door of the church.

Ralph whined, "I don't know. You know how they talk; it was tough for me to understand."

"Ralph, the guy's an Ivy League graduate and has more education than both of us put together, and in your case, that's not saying much. Don't tell me you couldn't understand him. It's more likely the other way around. Okay, so you didn't say anything to anyone about the T.A.R.P. funds?" J.R. let loose of Ralph's arm. "Then how could Quince find out? Witherspoon must have talked to him after talking to Olajuwon. This is getting out of hand."

J.R. looked up. Ralph was already entering the church.

Yusef Olajuwon

Chapter 16

J.R. entered the bank in a miserable mood, given that it was Monday and he had a long day and week ahead. His weekend was ruined when Sally refused to go to Chicago and got worse when Monica insisted he attend the dedication service at the Baptist church.

Walking across the lobby, he was his usual somber self until he noted his office door was open, unusual but not beyond expectation since the cleaning crew usually made their visit on Sunday and occasionally forgot to relock his office door. Sally was not at her desk—again, not an unusual occurrence. He entered the office and found Yusuf sitting in the over-stuffed chair and Sally holding cream and sugar while he mixed his coffee.

"Good morning, J.R. You have a guest," Sally said, retreating to the door and closing it as she exited.

Yusuf greeted him with a giant smile and a robust, "How are you this fine morning, Mr. Roberts? My, what a wonderful assistant you have. Very attentive, very professional."

"Is this like some kind of government conspiracy or something? Never calling for an appointment, or is it something they forgot to teach you at government employee school?" J.R. walked around his desk and stood next to his chair. "I'm really busy this morning, so why don't you go bother some of the staff, or better yet, just leave."

"J.R., you are a tough one. I won't take much of your time. Just checking to see how you're doing with the infusion of money. I note you have put some of it to work." He pulled out a sheaf of papers and studied it for a second. "You've made quite a score on the overnight and daily interest, and you have moved some of the money to First Fidelity for some short-term use. That's good." Yusuf set the papers in his lap and continued, "But you haven't applied yourself to the real reason for this program."

J.R. plopped down in his chair. "What? You want I should stand at the door and hand everyone that comes through a hundred-dollar bill?"

Yusuf chuckled. "In this small town, you would probably have them coming in for seconds before the day was done. No, that's not what I had in mind. I understand there's a big investor shopping around town for a place to build a hotel convention center."

"Oh, now it's a convention center. Last week, it was an amusement park. Next week, it will probably be some kind of professional sports arena, even though we don't have a professional team within two hundred miles. I can just see the private jets carrying the superstars circling aimlessly since we don't have a paved airport."

"You are a funny one, aren't you?" Yusuf's smile was gone. "Look, J.R., it's nice that you can sit around in your plush office, drive your expensive cars, holiday on your expensive yacht, and on and on, but this town is dying on the vine. If this guy is real, you need to talk to him and give him the support necessary to make this a reality, and this bank now has the means to do it."

"Let me get this straight. You are suggesting, insisting, that my bank give any drifter that meanders through this town a blank check, assuming he can spell whatever he says he wants to build, and my guess is that this guy can't. I've met him, and once you get by the fancy boots and the Stetson, believe me, there's not much there."

"Ah, you've met Mr. Quince. That's a start. Give it a chance, J.R. Maybe by next month's board meeting, we'll be discussing his loan." Yusuf got up, stretched. "I wish I could stay for lunch. I would love to take your assistant to your country club. I rather enjoyed my visit the other night. Perhaps you will invite me to play golf someday, J.R. That would be nice."

Chapter 17

Dr. Ruben Rubinski's waiting room was paneled in dark mahogany with recessed lighting, giving patrons a moment of relaxing meditation before entering the plush confines of the psychiatrist's den. J.R. leafed through a three-month-old edition of *Business Week,* skipping the article about the long-term expectations and effect of the troubled asset relief program.

A pleasant looking middle-aged woman stepped out of the inner exam room, tissue in hand, and black streams of mascara marring her surgically perfected complexion. She glanced at J.R., and he could only assume the vision of another man made her bring the tissue to her face again and gulp back a sob as she lunged for the exit.

Rubinski walked out of the inner room, and ignoring J.R., walked to his receptionist and whispered in her ear as she scribbled notes. At some point during the exchange, both cracked smiles and tried to withhold any obvious levity. J.R. imagined the conversation was about the prior patient and her husband's infidelity; discovering him in the act at some obscure motel in a most uncompromising position. The funny part was probably the doctor's description of the pictures that had been taken by her private detective.

The doctor disappeared into a back hallway, and the room once again went silent. J.R. was the only patient waiting for his appointment, which was now twenty minutes late. He stood, walked to the receptionist, and said, "Ahem," clearing his throat. He looked at his Rolex and continued, "Should we reschedule?"

The receptionist looked up and gave him an uninterested smile. "Dr. Rubinski is reviewing your file, preparing for your session. It will just be another minute." She held her fake smile as she looked down at a notepad full of scribbles.

J.R. returned to his seat, plopped down, and crossed his legs, tapping his fingers on his knee. This was his second session, the first forty-minute session taken up by a review of J.R.'s youthful experiences. He still didn't understand the significance. He had decided to seek professional help after his stuttering disorder reinvented itself. He figured he could get a professional opinion in a single session and maybe get some pills to help him control or eliminate his problem. Instead, he spent forty minutes talking about his youthful sexual inhibitions and other events that may have influenced his personality.

Rubinski had been recommended by his family physician, and with offices in Cougar Falls, he was far enough away to avoid being seen by any acquaintances. J.R.'s impatience apparently stimulated the receptionist to take some action. She made a call on her intercom and then said, "Mr. Roberts, you can go in now."

J.R. sighed in disgust, walked by without acknowledging her effort, and entered the interview room. Rubinski was seated in an overstuffed, mahogany leather chair a few feet from a matching couch. He was studying notes, and he looked up with the same smile as his receptionist and said, "Nice to see you, J.R. Have a seat, please." He was the picture of a late middle-aged physician, much as one would see on prime-time television—thick salt and pepper hair, lightly tanned complexion, with crow's feet at the corners of his contact-enhanced deep blue eyes. Half-glasses perched on the end of his nose. He dressed casually in chinos, loafers, and an open-neck oxford shirt with an expensive designer decal and sat, legs crossed, with no intention of rising to recognize J.R.'s entrance.

"Let's see, when we left off last time, we were dealing with your perplexed view of your father and some recognition of inferiority, but still-high esteem and gratitude. Would you like to continue from there?"

"My what?" J.R. responded in dismay. "I didn't say anything like that. We were talking about how I came to own the freaking bank. As I recall, one of the last things we talked about was whether you could buy any stock."

"J.R.," Rubinski said in a condescending voice, "it's my job to interpret what is said in these sessions. After we finish, I take considerable time to study my notes and the transcript to determine the problems we are facing. That's the purpose of these meetings—to get to the root of your disorder. Now, did you notice how easily you were disturbed by my comment?"

J.R. was tormented during these sessions with the urge to get up, smack the doctor in the nose and stomp out; the action would certainly help if not solve his disorder. "I don't think I am disturbed; I am just relating what I got out of the last session and the two hundred bucks I spent."

"Remember what I said when we started. I don't tolerate sarcasm and disdain for my profession—not because I can't take it, but because ninety percent of the patients I see don't think they need my services. They are here either at someone else's urging or to satisfy their own curiosity. Now, can we start again? What do you think causes your flash temper?"

Once again, J.R. thought, *Idiots like you*, but withheld the comment, sighed, and sat back in the chair. He talked for several minutes about the inner workings of the bank, thinking about the two hundred-dollar an hour meter that was ticking. "I'm under a lot of pressure. It's normal, I suppose, dealing with the bank and all of the government regulations; sometimes it just gets to be too much."

"Go on," Rubinski urged.

"What's there to go on about? You have what, one employee, and I have thirty. Hell, one employee likes to peek in windows and play with himself while he's doing it, and I have to deal with that."

This comment made Rubinski look up from his notes. "Why don't you fire him? Sounds like reasonable grounds."

"It's a lot more complicated than that."

"You mean there are other complications that may result from your action?"

J.R. sensed a trap. "Maybe."

"Like what?"

"There are all kinds of things when you fire someone. That's why I have an H.R. person."

"So, you really don't have to deal with it. You just choose to."

J.R. started to get irritated again. "I'm the president of the bank; I have to be involved. When the lawsuit arrives at the door, guess whose name is on it?"

"I would guess you have insurance for that sort of thing. Do you see where I'm going here, J.R.? Actually, where you are leading us."

J.R. suppressed the urge to respond with sarcasm and said, "No, I really don't. Are you telling me I'm a poor manager?"

"So far, J.R., most or all of the problems we have talked about are things you could delegate to someone else. You choose to deal with them internally, let them gnaw at you while you accumulate more. The mind and body can only take so much before they erupt in some unpleasant way. If it's physical intake—food or drink—you vomit to get rid of the poison. If it's mental overload, something far more disturbing happens. In your case, it's stuttering, and it could get worse, like a complete mental breakdown. The stuttering is just a preliminary symptom of something worse."

"So, you are suggesting I need a vacation or something?"

Now Rubinski sighed. "No, J.R., I was just highlighting something obvious that I am sure you already know. My guess is that there are some issues far more disconcerting to you that you are withholding, but our time is dwindling. I think we made progress today." He glanced at his watch and scribbled some notes on his pad. "Anything you want to discuss in these last few minutes? I'm curious. How did you discover that this employee likes to peek in windows?"

J.R. had to be truthful; after all, this guy spent his whole career pinning people down for lying. "He had to go to court, so I checked on the outcome."

"Really? And did he get convicted?"

"Yeah, he got fined, and the judge gave him a verbal reprimand."

"Who was he spying on? Was this a crime of passion? I mean, like someone he knew? You know, someone he works with or something?"

J.R. stared at Rubinski like a cat with a mouthful of mice, dumbfounded. How did the conversation get so out of hand so quick? How did this shrink put everything together after just two questions? It had to be coincidental. "I-I d-d-don't know."

Rubinski's head jerked up, and he gave J.R. a penetrating stare. "You don't know, or you don't want to say? Well, we have come to the precipice, haven't we? We can either jump, or step back and continue to wonder what to do next. In any event, we certainly have a good starting point for the next session, wouldn't you agree?"

Murt Featherstone

CHAPTER 18

Bit stood at the counter of the county recorder's office, Stetson in hand, waiting for someone to address his inquiry. Muriel Featherstone slowly rose from her swivel chair, groaning as she extricated her plus-sized rear end from between the armrests. Bit gave her a big smile and said, "How we doin' today—" He hesitated, trying to see the engraved nameplate on her desk, "Muriel? Muriel Featherstone. I had an uncle that went by the name Featherstone. He was quarter-Apache and a mess of other things." Bit saw that his inquiry about her ancestry was not being received well, so he changed the subject. "I'm thinking about buying some land out near the interchange and would like to see the plat map for that area. I'm told you are the person I need to talk to, Muriel."

"I go by Murt," Muriel said without returning the smile. She was about forty with short, dark hair frizzed up in the front, forming a large curl above her forehead that reminded Bit of the McDonald's golden arch. Her one-piece flowered dress had

FIRST STATE BANK and (dis)TRUST of Hinkley County

fashionable doily lace around the neckline and on both cuffs, reminiscent of a square dancing outfit Bit's mother used to wear on Saturday nights. Her complexion, puffy cheeks, and plump physique completed the picture of a healthy country girl.

"You be the guy they are all talkin' about?" Murt asked.

"I guess that depends on what they are saying. If they're saying, 'He's one heck of nice guy,' or 'That dude could coax a mare out of her Sunday saddle,' I might be the guy." Bit rested his elbow on the counter and leaned toward Murt.

"Said you was a sweet talker; guess they was right." Murt waddled over to the swinging door separating the reception area from the main office and, opening the door, invited Bit to step in. "My brother's a county commissioner, you know. He's the one told me there was some hotshot cowboy roamin' around town, talkin' about buildin' some kind of amusement park." Murt laughed as she led Bit to an open area with a large rectangular table, turned, and said, "You don't look stupid, but looks are deceiving sometimes."

Bit smiled and said, "Murt, I haven't met too many smart people in Hinkley up to this point; you may be the exception to the rule."

Murt smiled for the first time. She walked over to a wall lined with deep shelving and ran her hand along the books until she came to her target. She pulled the large, bound manuscript out, the dust billowing up. She laid the large book down on the table and began paging through maps until she grunted and said, "Here you are—range ten, section twenty-three." She ran her finger along a straight line on the map. "That's the four-lane, east to west, and here's where it meets Route 27, or Main Street. Great place for an amusement park," she said with some sarcasm.

"Just between you and me, Murt, I ain't buildin' any amusement park. Don't exactly know how that rumor got started. Was thinkin' about a motel of some sort, maybe with one of those big water slide things. Something for the kids, you know?" Bit stepped a little closer to Murt. "You have any kids, Murt?"

Murt's smile got bigger. "No, I never been married. Not the marryin' kind, I guess. Now that you mention it, a motel with a cement swimmin' hole might be nice. There's the municipal pool over by the school, but with all the rules they have, ain't much fun. Can't run, can't drink, can't swim after dark; can't do nothin' kids like to do. Adults, neither. So, a swimmin' hole might be nice."

"Murt, me and you, we think alike. Now—" Bit looked a little closer at the map. "This piece here, the one next to the highway that's all squared up, who owns that?"

Murt drew close to Bit, her hand touching his as she pointed at the spot on the map. "This one here? That's Henry Thornberry's farm. He owns on the other side of the highway, too. It got split when they put the four-lane in. Been in his family for over a hundred and fifty years; they homesteaded here. They were original settlers, along with the Hinkleys."

"You don't say." Bit rested his hand on Murt's shoulder. "You think he'd ever sell a chunk of that corner? Make a fine place for a swimmin' hole."

"Don't know about that. I mean, I know old man Thornberry. See him every Sunday at church. He don't have no family around here any more. After his wife died, his daughter up and ran off with the Flannery kid. That was a long time ago. He lives in a big house there on the farm, the other side of the road. You probably saw it when you came into town."

"You think if I showed up at church, you could introduce me to Mr. Thornberry?" Bit helped Murt put the book back on the shelf, leaning over her as they lifted it back in place, his groin rubbing against her protruding hindquarter.

Murt groaned as she turned, leaned against the shelf, and grabbed the lapels of Bit's coat, pulling him close.

Bit resisted, but gave her a big smile. "Slow down now, Murt; this just might get you in trouble, you bein' the sister of the commissioner and all." Murt panted and groaned again. "How about I meet you at church this Sunday? We talk to Mr. Thornberry and then, I don't know, we'll see what happens after that."

Bit pulled back, and Murt stepped away from the shelves, brushed her flowered dress with her hands, and sucked in a big breath of air.

FIRST STATE BANK and (dis)TRUST of Hinkley County

"You stayin' somewheres close to town?" Murt asked as she continued to brush imaginary dust from her dress. "I could meet you and, you know, show you the farm. I mean all of the farm," she added seductively.

Bit asked, "Which church we talkin' about?"

Murt sighed. "The Body of Christ on the Cross Baptist Church, on Maple Street."

"Ah, yes, Pastor Butterbetter."

"You know Pastor Butterbetter?"

"Not exactly," Bit responded, "but I'll be lookin' for you after church. Thanks for your help and all the information. You've been a peach." Bit started for the exit, Murt trailing behind.

"Do you want me to meet you before?"

"No darlin'. I'm not sure what time I can get there. I'll find you. Don't you worry your little—uh, so just don't worry."

Sunday was a special day in Sally's life. Everyone left for church, and for most of the day, she had the parsonage to herself. Now that they had moved next door into the new parsonage, which included a Jacuzzi bathtub, she could lounge with the music of her choice turned up and not worry about disturbing Pastor Butterbetter's meditation as he prepared for his Sunday sermon.

Since turning twenty-one, she had expressed her independence by not attending church on a regular basis, much to the pastor's displeasure, but she continued to live in his house as long as she followed certain rules and those rules did not interfere with her social agenda.

The sun was high and warm, and Sally sat on the back porch of the new house wearing a modest two-piece swimsuit, the maximum exhibition allowed in the Butterbetter household. The bells hanging in the church bell tower tolled the conclusion of the Sunday morning service, and Sally's younger sister bounced up the steps of the porch and stopped next to Sally, panting from the run across the parking lot.

"Man, you missed it?"

Sally had dark, wide-rimmed Marilyn Monroe sunglasses on and didn't turn her head from the sun when responding. "Missed what? Mrs. Riley collapse in the choir loft again?"

"The guy everyone is talking about, the amusement park guy—he was at church. Sat right in the front, like he was part of the family. You talk about a stud."

Sally sat up and lifted her legs off the lounge chair so fast the chair partially collapsed, trapping her in the fold. As she fought to extricate herself she said, "Who? Bit was in the church, today?"

"I didn't say anyone got bit, I said—"

Sally interrupted harshly, "What did he look like? Was he tall, tanned, and wearing cowboy boots, like some kind of movie star?"

"Yeah, only better."

Sally jumped up, ran off the porch, and peeked around the corner of the house into the church parking lot. She turned back to her sister. "Did you see him leave?"

"What are you so jumpy about? Think he's gonna get exited because you got your tits all bunched up in that tight swimmin' suit?"

"Shut up. Did you see him leave?" Sally asked sternly.

Her sister now knew she had some valuable information and leaned against the porch rail gaining some attitude. "I didn't see him leave because he ain't left yet."

Sally ran back to the porch and grabbed her sister's arm. "So where is he? Is he still inside? What's he there for? Who's he talking to?"

Her sister pulled away, brushing off her grasp, and responded indignantly, "I don't know what he's doing. He was talking to some old man and Murt Featherstone. She was flitting around like a prairie chicken protecting a nest. You'd-a thought she had somethin' goin' with him. I mean, like that's a possibility."

Sally ran into the house, grabbing any clothes she could find, and dressed while rushing for the front door. Halfway down the front steps she realized she was barefoot and had to dash back inside and find suitable foot attire to accompany her choice of clothing. Settling on a pair of black stilettos, she stumbled down the steps and clumsily rushed across the parking lot, running her fingers through her hair in a desperate attempt to clear the tangles.

Bit stood near the front of the sanctuary, surrounded by interested townspeople trying to listen in on his conversation with Henry Thornberry. Murt had her arm looped through Bit's as they talked to Thornberry, and Pastor Butterbetter was in the group as well, shaking hands and tending his flock. Sally approached with caution, making her way down the outside aisle, trying to make eye contact with Bit.

"Why, Miss Butterbetter, it's so nice to see you. I looked all over during the service, but didn't see you. Mother, it's Miss Butterbetter; isn't that nice?" Pucker stood behind Sally, and Edna looked around him from behind his shoulder with a broad smile on her face.

Sally turned, nodded, and said, "Hi, Pucker. I don't have time right now, okay? So, uh, hi, Edna. Could we do this later?" Sally looked at Bit and could tell the meeting was starting to break up, although Murt had not released her hold on his arm.

Edna said, "We was thinking, Sally, that maybe you would like to go to the Denny's with us for lunch. They've got a fruit and salad bar, you know. I mean, not that you would have to just eat fruit and salad. Ernest will get you anything you want." She smiled again and poked Pucker in the back.

"Yeah, anything you want," Pucker said apprehensively.

Sally stared in disbelief. "Uh, not today, okay? Sounds nice, the salad bar and all, but I've something else I have to do."

Bit turned, trying to release himself from Murt, so Sally made her move, cutting across the aisles.

Pucker yelled at her back, "Nice to see you, Miss Butterbetter. Maybe next week."

Pucker's good-bye echoed off the walls of the church and the remaining few turned to see Sally stumble through the tight pew, catching her clothing on misplaced hymnals. She stopped, pulling at her dress, which had tangled in a hymnal holder and smiled, holding herself up with one hand and expelling a big breath blowing hair out of her face. She cracked a smile attempting but not succeeding to be inconspicuous.

Bit said, "How y'all doin' today?"

Murt said in a low, gurgling voice, "It's that Butterbetter girl."

Pastor Butterbetter said, "Sally, you're just in time to help gather the communion trays."

Henry Thornberry growled, "I need a drink."

The rest of the crowd turned and headed for the exit.

Murt decided to help clean up the communion trays and leave Bit to his business with Thornberry. Sally ignored her father's request and followed Bit and Thornberry to the door leading to the parking lot along with the last few members of the congregation.

Bit shook Thornberry's hand and said, "I'll take you up on that drink on your front porch, Mr. Thornberry, just as soon as I get through talking to the little lady here."

Bit put his hat on, touched his finger to the bill in salutation to the others, and walked over to Sally, who was trying to act uninterested next to Bit's parked Cadillac.

"Didn't see you in church today, or I would have had a seat right next to you. Course, ol' Murt probably woulda had to be between us, but all in a day's work."

"And what kind of work would that be?" Sally said crossing her arms with attitude.

Bit smiled back. "Well, now, that's kind of a complicated subject, not suitable for a Sunday afternoon. Sundays are for long walks, swingin' on porch swings, and just enjoying the day. Don't you think so?"

"I think a lot of things, but you and Murt Featherstone, that's a thought I never would have imagined."

"Oh, now, don't get your feathers all up over nothin'," Bit said casually. "Ol' Murt was just doin' me a favor. Nice lady. Knows a lot about the lay of the land around here. Now I have to go talk to Henry Thornberry. Won't take too long, and it might involve a drink or two. Says he has some spiked lemonade that will take the shine off a pair of new boots, but once I get that out of the way, what say you and I go find one of those porch swings and enjoy this Sunday afternoon."

Sally studied Bit. A tingle in her spine made her twitch. "Uh, I guess that would be nice. What swing are you referring to?"

"Well, that's a good question." Bit pondered for a moment and said, "Better yet, maybe we could just take a walk around Thornberry's place. Have a picnic. Sound nice?"

Sally's mouth dried up, and her train of thought was interrupted by scenes of blankets lying next to a cool stream, wine glasses and woven picnic baskets under a shade tree. "I-I-I'll bring lunch and meet you there in an hour."

"You are a peach, Sally Butterbetter."

CHAPTER 19

Roger Witherspoon swept through Ralphy's front door, disengaging himself from his suit coat as he made a beeline to the end barstool. Ralphy stood behind the bar, funneling quarters into a paper coin roll.

"Just talked to Murt Featherstone," Witherspoon said, placing his hands on the bar in anticipation of his first glass of beer.

"She still have that hair thing going on? You know—that big curl on her forehead?" Ralphy threw the rolled quarters in a bag and pulled a cold mug from the cooler.

"Dumb question, I think she had the same dress on she wore when we were in high school. Anyway, I heard Quince was snooping around the courthouse, so I asked Murt. She's gossip central over there, and she said he was in her office looking at plot maps. I only got that out of her after she told me they have a thing going. Seriously, she hinted that they were meeting on the sly wherever he's staying, but wouldn't say where that was, of course. She'll never change. She'd drop her drawers right here on the bar if you promised to take her to the soda fountain after."

Witherspoon took a long draw on his beer and then shoved the empty glass across the bar to Ralphy. "Anyway, I was able to get her to tell me what he was looking at. He's looking at the Thornberry place, out near the interchange."

"Makes sense," Ralphy said, drawing Witherspoon another beer. "I don't suspect he'll have much luck with Henry, though. I heard when they put the interchange in he ran the oil company reps off with a shotgun. Said he wasn't gonna have lights shinin' in his windows all night. Remember? They had to take the middle of his farm by immaculate… Uh—immaculate do—you know what I mean."

"Imminent domain. I remember that. I was in college, but my old man mentioned it."

"As I recall—" Ralphy rested his elbow on the bar. "They even moved the highway over a hundred yards so he could keep his house. They wanted to move the house and barns—make it look exactly the same, only a hundred yards south. He wouldn't have none of it. It's coming back now. I remember. Judge Hinkley was still on the bench, and the trial was a big deal. Back then, they still printed the paper every day, and everybody was following it. The state suit—I mean attorney—made his case for movin' the house, saying it was for the public good and that the highway would create all these jobs, make everyone within five hundred miles rich, garbage like that. I think your old man, John Witherspoon, represented Henry. All I remember is that when your dad was done, Old Hinkley said, 'If the state wants to put a highway in, they better figure out a way to go around Henry's house.'"

"No kidding? My dad represented Thornberry, huh?"

"You probably have the records somewheres down in the basement. Anyway, I think Henry even gave the land to the state after they struck the deal to curve the highway around his house."

"Damn, I really need to talk to this Quince guy. If he's going to talk to Thornberry, that's an easy in for me—our firm representing Thornberry in the biggest land deal of the last century."

J.R Roberts

CHAPTER 20

J.R. sat in Dr. Rubinski's consultation room, his arms crossed in defiance, sweat gathering on his brow. The distaste he had acquired for the man during the first two visits had now grown into hatred.

Rubinski had just asked if J.R. had experienced any tense events over the past week that may have triggered his speech impediment. J.R. had sarcastically answered that his whole life was a tense event.

"J.R., we all feel our lives are filled with drama and things beyond our control, but after a little contemplation, most of those events are trivial when compared to what really matters. So tell me, what are some of the problems that you feel are so insurmountable."

J.R. took a big breath, contemplated the question, and thought of leaving. He thought of throwing the paperweight that sat on the coffee table between them and a few other undesirable outcomes, and then decided he was paying the idiot for the session and it was completely confidential, so why not?

"Well, to start with, my girlfriend suddenly decided our relationship is too, too—too something, I don't know—too potentially dangerous since the Pucker kid caught us screwing at the Best Western. Then there's the Treasury Department African guy that keeps trying to pressure me into making loans to some cowboy drifter that wants to build an amusement park and convention center in a town that doesn't have enough stoplights to qualify for a spot on the state road map. My wife thinks the bank is her personal savings account, my kids think American Express is my mailing address and, well, you get the ugly picture." J.R. sank back in the chair, realizing he felt better now that he had regurgitated his most sensitive problems, even though there was little chance an over-priced, over-educated shrink could do anything about it.

"Let's start with the girlfriend. Obviously, you have a more complex relationship than you have previously talked about if you are having conjugal meetings. Will this relationship lead to the disillusion of your marriage?"

"Of course not," J.R. retorted in a patronizing manner. "She's just one of my emp—she's just a friend and maybe I let things get out of hand. I will fix it; I just have to be careful."

"Careful? Why?"

"You have all of those credentials hanging on the wall and you ask a question like that?" J.R. leaned forward, staring at Rubinski.

"J.R., remember the rules. I ask the questions, and you try to give sincere answers. You are the one with the problems, and you have come to me for help. Besides, someone needs to ask simple questions, ones you seem to avoid." Rubinski scribbled more notes.

"I have to be careful because women tend to get pissed off when you dump them, and they do stupid things—like tell your wife." J.R. crossed his arms again, ready to confront the next question.

"Sounds more like she is dumping you. Does that cause you concern?"

"She has too much to lose to dump me," J.R. responded, much more reposed and staring at the wall.

"You mean like material things? Gifts and such?"

"Well, yeah, things like that."

"Maybe her job?" Rubinski looked up from his notes over his half-glasses.

J.R. didn't say anything, but for the first time looked at his watch, hoping the session was ending.

There was a lingering lull and then Rubinski continued, "There seems to be a pattern here. Do you see it?"

"Can't say I do, but then, you are the shrink—doctor. What's the pattern?"

"I could give you a lot of medical jargon, use a lot of psychological terms, but let's make this easy; you're your own worse enemy. A common metaphor, but appropriate in this case." Rubinski scribbled some more notes.

"I paid two hundred bucks for you to tell me that?"

"No, you paid me two hundred bucks to tell yourself that. You came here because you thought you had a problem that could be fixed with drugs. You might have even had some inkling that counseling might work. You did not come here to evaluate your life and inner psyche. But regardless of what you wanted, you are making progress." Rubinski looked at his watch for the first time. "We have a few minutes left; tell me about the issue at the bank. Do you feel frightened by the African guy? Do you feel frightened by people of color in general?"

"Of course not. I'm not frightened. I'm just frustrated. You don't understand what it's like to deal with people that live off the government. They think they are superior and we are subservient."

"You use generalities like 'them' and 'they' when you refer to this person. How do you think he feels about you?" Scribble, scribble.

"You are inferring that I am prejudiced in some way, and that's not true. The guy barged into my office and inserted himself

FIRST STATE BANK and (dis)TRUST of Hinkley County

into my business, using the government as a tool. It's not right. Even more than that, it's not legal. I have my attorney working on it now." J.R. looked at his watch. "Are we done?"

"Only you can answer that."

Sally Butterbetter

Chapter 21

Bit sat next to Sally's desk in the bank lobby, legs crossed, hat on his lap, his hands folded, waiting for either J.R. or Sally to make an appearance. Sally stepped out of the employee lounge, straightening her calf-length black skirt and adjusting the collar of her silken blouse. Pucker noticed her entrance from his teller station and straightened, cleared his throat, and addressed Sally. "Good morning, Miss Butterbetter."

Sally looked at Pucker, sighed, and wandered over to his station. "Hi, Pucker. Have all your pencils sharpened?"

Pucker smiled broadly, thoroughly infatuated with the fact that Sally had responded to his greeting, regardless of the content. Sally leaned her elbow on the counter in front of Pucker, her back turned to him as he said, "My, you do look nice—"

Sally saw Bit sitting in the lobby and walked away from Pucker in mid-sentence.

Bit stood and said, "How you doin' this mornin', darlin'? You know, you're prettier than a spring cactus flower."

FIRST STATE BANK and (dis)TRUST of Hinkley County

Sally blushed as she absorbed the compliment. "Uh, I—Hi, Bit. What are you doing here?" Sally frowned, disappointed with her response and wanting to back up and start over.

"I'm glad you asked. I'm waiting for J.R. We have a little business to discuss. You know—the Thornberry thing. You suppose he will be around soon? By the way, that picnic was more fun than a box of baby rabbits. I still don't know how you put all those fancy fixin's together so fast. And wine glasses to boot. You are somethin', Sally Butterbetter."

Sally stood with her mouth open in an expression similar to Pucker's just a few moments before. "Uh, thank you. It wasn't anything." There was an uncomfortable second, and Sally continued, "J.R.—he'll be here soon. He called earlier and said he had to deal with some issues at home, something about an interior decorator that was charging too much. Every time his wife gets upset with him, she calls this interior designer from Chicago to come down and redecorate one of the rooms. So, are you in town for a while?"

"Well, now." Bit stepped a little closer. "Long enough to spend some time with you. How about we try that lunch spot again? I got a hankerin' for more of that chili."

Sally, her body now the consistency of a damp washcloth, stared up at Bit with longing eyes and did not notice J.R. stomping across the lobby.

"Am I interrupting something?" J.R. said harshly, breaking the spell.

Sally stepped back, adjusting her blouse, and said, "Mr. Quince is here to see you."

"I can see that, Sally," J.R. responded in a condescending tone. "As usual, Quince, you didn't have the courtesy to make an appointment, but I suppose that's not the cowboy way."

Bit smiled broadly. "J.R., you are a serious one, aren't you? No, I was just around town, gettin' the feel of the place, and I thought, Bit, why don't you stop in and see how ol' J.R. is doin'. You know what I mean? Just a friendly visit. And there's some business that might be worth talkin' about, if you've got the time."

J.R. gave Sally a severe glance, turned, and started for his office. "Come on; let's get this friendly visit over with. I've got things to do."

Bit smiled at Sally and winked, following J.R. into the office and closing the door behind him.

"How we doin' this mornin', J.R.? Havin' problems at home? That's a shame. You have to keep an eye on those big city boys. Before you know it, they're into your back pocket faster than a carnival pick pocket."

"What?" J.R. said with disdain and shaking his head. "Sally doesn't know how to keep her mouth shut. Besides wanting to nose around in my personal business, Mr. Quince, what's this visit all about?"

"Always wanting to get right down to business. You are a serious one, J.R. You better be careful. That can cause stomach ulcers. You know, my daddy always said, 'If you can't enjoy the day, there ain't much use gettin' outta bed.'"

"My guess is your daddy didn't run a bank. Now, can we get this over with?"

Bit leaned back in the plush chair, rubbing the leather armrests in admiration. "This is a fine piece of furniture. Sturdy, if you know what I mean. That expensive designer guy get you this? I might be able to use him when I decorate the lobby of the hotel."

"Still going on about the motel amusement park deal, huh? You know, I give you credit. You do know how to stir up people's interest. You are the talk of the town, even if it's all hogwash."

Bit smiled, adjusted his shoulders, and said, "Here's where we are, J.R. I took an option on ol' Thornberry's place—the half opposite his house at the intersection. He wouldn't have any talk of movin'. I have Murt Featherstone pulling all of the information together at the courthouse so I can get the land deal done. It's already approved for commercial development; the carpetbaggers saw to that thirty years ago when they were anticipating the highway goin' through. I have my site man flying over in the sputter bug to take aerials and review the topography."

"In the what?" J.R. said, looking up from his laptop.

"The sputter bug. Helicopter. You want to take a ride? I can have him land right here in the bank parkin' lot. That'd be a hoot, wouldn't it? I bet Sally would really get a kick out of that."

J.R. tried to withhold his inquisitive enthusiasm, but couldn't help asking, "You own a helicopter?"

"Well, 'own' might be a stretch. I try not to own too many things, but the sputter bug is a nice toy when you want to get places in a hurry and there ain't no roads. My pilot owns the thing, and I just rent it when there's a need, like today."

J.R. sat back and studied Bit, thinking maybe he had underestimated the man, then shrugged it off and went back to studying his computer screen.

"You heard anything from Yusuf? Has he been urging you to get on board with this project?" Bit nonchalantly reached over and set his hat on the floor next to the chair.

J.R. became alert and stared at Bit. "Where did you get that name?"

"A fellow spreads some money around, and it's amazing what information turns up. I understand he's close to the bank now, right there with the decision makers, if you know what I mean."

J.R. felt his blood pressure rising. "No, I don't know what you mean, so if you are driving at some point, let's get to it."

"Well, is he is, or is he ain't. That's pretty simple, I'd say. I heard he's on your board and he's gonna be helping with decisions about loans and all. Since I'm linin' up to get a loan, I'm askin' if he and you are in cahoots decidin' who gets what." Bit put a little crease in his voice.

"First of all, Mr. Quince," J.R. said with authority, pointing his finger at Bit. "Don't use that tone of voice in this office, or you may find yourself sitting on the parking lot curb. Second, Olajuwon may think he's some kind of big shot around here, but he's not; he's nothing more than another government scab that attaches itself to the rear end of the machines that make this economic engine turn. And third, I'm getting ready to scratch that scab off and pitch it in the trash, and if you are not careful, you may find yourself in the same pile."

Bit smiled and relaxed. "Sounds like you aren't too fond of Mr. Olajuwon."

"Let's quit the cat and mouse game, Mr. Quince. Tell me where we are going."

Bit chewed his lip for a second and said, "I think I'm goin' to lunch, and if you don't mind, I think I'm gonna take that little number sittin' at that desk out there with me. When I get the final numbers together on this deal, I'll be back, and I hope you have your checkbook open and ready." He stood up, stretched, and looked toward the door. "You don't mind if Miss Sally joins me for lunch, do you, J.R.? Strictly business."

J.R.'s blood pressure was peaking, and his face showed it. He responded with deadpan lack of sincerity. "I guess that's up to her."

Bit and Sally walked down the street toward Ralphy's, the mid-day sun penetrating their light clothing. Bit carried his coat over his shoulder, and Sally struggled to keep her balance in three-inch heels.

"Ol' J.R. seemed a little tense today. You do that to him?" Bit tipped his hat at a couple passing on the sidewalk.

"Me? I don't have any control over his moods. It's mostly his wife. As I said, she decided to decorate, upset over something he did, or something she thinks he did, and that ruined his day. Believe me, she knows which buttons to push." Sally stopped, grabbed Bit's arm for balance, and took her shoes off. "God, I don't know why I wear these things. You don't mind, do you?"

"Honey, the more you take off, the happier I am."

Reaching the front door of Ralphy's, Bit took the lead, entering the darkness of the restaurant. The crowd hushed as they entered, but returned to the hum of unrecognizable conversation soon after. Bit's presence was becoming more commonplace in the small community. Sally leaned on the door jam, sliding her feet into the demon shoes.

Bit led Sally to an empty booth and sat down, offering her his trademark smile. "J.R. didn't seem none too happy when I told him about my lunch plans."

"Bet not. He's been a little moody lately." Sally did not make eye contact.

"You have anything to do with his moodiness?"

Sally looked up from her water glass. "He may find my lack of interest a little disturbing."

"Wow, that sounds like lawyer talk. It's just you and me talkin' here, darlin'. It ain't like I don't know what's been goin' on. You're all growed up and know what you want and how to get it, so it ain't gonna surprise me, no matter what you say."

Sally contemplated the request and then said, "He's under a lot of pressure, and I told him we should cool it for a while."

Bit smiled, apparently liking her answer. Movement in the entranceway caught his attention, and he noted another tall figure entering the restaurant, silhouetted in the bright light.

Sheriff Reginald Cornwallace Miner stepped just inside the doorway and stopped, allowing his eyes to adjust to the dim light. He wore a broad-brimmed Stetson, a well-pressed black uniform shirt with sheriff decals on the shoulders, and creased chinos just lapping over his shiny wellingtons. He was the perfect picture of small-town law enforcement, and the way the conversational undertone of the restaurant dulled as he moved through the tables alluded to his power.

Miner smiled and spoke frequently to patrons as he moved from table to table, patting people on the back, shaking hands, giving an occasional expression of concern, padding his political tab with every greeting.

Miner eventually made his roundabout way to Bit and Sally conversing in the booth. "Sally Butterbetter, it's been quite a while, and I must say you have turned into quite a beautiful young lady. How is Pastor Butterbetter? And Mrs. Butterbetter? And young Emily? I bet she's every bit as lovely as you. What is she now, almost sixteen?"

Sally started to answer, trying to chronicle all of the questions and keep them in order.

"And who might this gentleman be? I don't think we've met, Mr. Quince." Miner didn't offer his hand.

Bit smiled broadly. "License tags are a good source of information, right, Sheriff?" Bit winked at Sally as she instinctively slid further into the booth away from the sheriff.

"Well, it's our job to keep an eye on vehicles with out-of-state plates, and yours is pretty easy to spot. You stayin' long, or are you just passin' through? You know, we don't take much to carpetbaggers around here, spreadin' rumors and takin' advantage of our friendly nature. You know what I mean?"

Bit smiled and again winked at Sally, laying his arm over the back of the booth and looking up at Miner. "I can understand that, Sheriff. A man like you gots to keep track of a lot of things—kids takin' pumpkins out of the pumpkin patch and such, so keepin' track of me is probably enough to put a man on edge. Would it help if I just checked in with you every once in a while? Then you wouldn't have to waste your time followin' me."

Miner's expression didn't change from his mild smirk. Miner bent a little closer to Bit's face and said in a flat, low tone, "Mr. Quince, you may think you can pull this flim-flam bullshit on the people of this town, and I'm sure some of them want to believe you because there ain't a whole lot to believe in right now, but I don't buy into your con. So remember, when you get ready to set the hook, I'm going to be there, only I'll be the one reelin' you in."

Miner stood up straight and looked at Sally with a more relaxed smile. "You might want to think better about the company you keep." Tipping the edge of his Stetson in salutation, he said, "Miss Butterbetter," and turned and walked toward the door.

Chapter 22

Bit read his last e-mail and was about to close his laptop and head for the shower. His cell buzzed, and he hit the intercept on the laptop and plugged the cell into the terminal to record the call before flipping open and answering. "Quince here."

"Mr. Quince, this is Terry Myers, personal assistant for Mr. Olajuwon. Thank you for taking my call. Have I caught you at a bad time?"

"I guess that depends on what you are calling about."

"Mr. Olajuwon asked me to contact you to see how your project is progressing. Our department is very interested in any new investment that creates jobs. That is our number one priority."

"I guess you can report that things are progressing," Bit responded.

"Have you started the financing process yet?"

"What's it to you, if I may ask?"

FIRST STATE BANK and (dis)TRUST of Hinkley County

"I think that is an area where we could be very helpful. Mr. Olajuwon works closely with entrepreneurs, helping them secure advantageous financing packages for their projects. Given the current tight credit market, you may find it difficult securing a loan. We can help, and in your case, I think we can guarantee a hundred percent success."

Bit let the silence linger for a long minute.

"Still there, Mr. Quince?"

"You have me hooked. How are you going to make these miracles happen?"

"That part doesn't need to be discussed at this point, but if you agree to the terms of our relationship, you will have no problems with the financing."

"Well, I guess we have arrived at the critical question. What does Mr. Olajuwon want to perform this miracle financing? I'm sure it's not just a hand shake and satisfaction his efforts created a few jobs." Bit smiled. He knew what was coming next.

"There is a modest fee involved, but it can be wrapped right into the financing package."

"A little vague, don't you think? A modest fee? We might have a different idea of what a modest fee is."

"We assess fifteen percent of the total package. But it's wrapped into the package so you can pass it on to the end user, just another professional fee mixed in with architect and engineering fees."

Bit thought, *This guy sounds more and more like a telephone solicitor selling vacation packages,* and then said, "Only a modest fee? Let's see. I'm mathematically challenged, but fifteen percent of eight million is pretty close to a million, right? Ol' Mr. Olajuwon walks away with a cool million for puttin' the strong arm on a local banker."

"I think that may be a poor characterization. Mr. Olajuwon works with local bankers and authorities to make sure you have a clear path to success. Why don't you think about it? I think after you have consulted with the bankers on your own, you will realize our offer is quite appealing."

The caller left his personal number and e-mail address for Bit to get back to him, along with a warning that the offer may disappear if action was not taken soon.

Bit hung up smiling and said to himself, "Gotcha."

Part II

Chapter 23

The president sat behind his large desk, the White House lawn and garden picturesque behind his plush reclining leather chair. He leaned his head against his thumb and finger, his arm supported by the chair, smiling an intriguing half-smile, hiding his thoughts as he waited for an answer to his inquiry about the state of the T.A.R.P. program. The meeting had covered numerous topics, but boiled down to a bull session on how to get the program out of the doldrums of bureaucratic regulation.

"Okay, Tim, we are almost a year into this program. Only a third of the funds have been allocated, and my numbers are starting to reflect disappointment among the very people that got me into this position. So, what's the deal? Can't you get your department in order? While you are trying to hire assistants, my poll numbers are shrinking faster than Barny Frank's testicles. What are we going to do? Or should I say, what are you going to do?"

Geithner scooted out on the edge of his chair, keeping a grasp on his paperwork. With a pencil in his hand as a prop, he responded, "Uh, I think we have a plan—a way to solve some of the public relations issues."

A hidden door on the far side of the room opened, and Michelle Obama stepped out, dressed in a nightgown with fluffy pink slippers, her hair in huge straightening rollers.

"Oh, I'm sorry. I thought you said you would be working alone. Hi, Tim." She stepped back inside the door so only her head was visible. "Uh, the dog peed on the floor again. I thought they said he was house trained."

The president had not moved, his head still supported by the same finger and thumb. "What do you want me to do? Come upstairs and kick him? Get security to take him out or to the kennel for the day. The girls are gone, aren't they?"

Geithner looked down, studying his notes, and remained silent.

Michelle looked sternly in the president's direction and vanished.

"See, Tim? That's what public relations will get you—a freaking dog that pees on the floor, and not just any floor—a four-hundred-thousand-dollar antique Persian rug presented to Teddy Roosevelt by the king of Siam, or maybe it was Yule Brenner. I don't know. Where were we?"

"Well, uh, we have developed a plan that I think will give us, well, a good opportunity to show what the program is supposed to do."

A mild hum emanated from somewhere within the maze of electronic communication equipment stuffed into the president's desk. Without moving the hand that supported his head, the president pushed a button. "Yes, what is it?"

There was a mumble of communication.

"I need another ten minutes. Tell Biden's people I'll call them back. Is this about that invitation to go fishing or sailing or something?"

Mumble, mumble, mumble.

"I don't do boats. I thought I made that clear."

Mumble, mumble.

"Okay, I'll get back to him, but schedule something so I don't have to even consider it."

He hit the button again and looked at Geithner. "So, what is this plan, and who came up with it?"

"Well, it was actually one of the interns in the office. We were talking about the, well, not failure, but the lack of impact the T.A.R.P. program was having, and Sheila—she's an intern from Georgetown—said, 'Why not emphasize the successes of the program? Maybe some of the other banks would get in line and, uh, you know, try to work through the program.' After thinking about it for a while—I think it might work."

The president listened, but his expression implied the idea didn't make an impact.

"Anyway, we threw the idea around, and it started to take shape. It, you know, kind of grew. We thought, well, if we want this thing to really get some legs, why not go right to Middle America? Then we thought, why not your home state? Find a bank that jumped on the program, prospered, and helped their community and the country, and make a big deal out of it." Geithner leaned back in his chair, feeling he had prosecuted his idea in good form. He twirled his pencil like a baton.

For the first time, the president sat up out of his slouch, surveyed the paperwork on his desk, looked at Geithner, and said, "I like it. Have you found a bank? I'd stay away from Chicago."

"Well, uh, we haven't taken it that far yet. I wanted to get your reaction—, I mean opinion—since, uh, we think you will probably want to participate in some way—maybe a visit, meet the bank management, that sort of thing."

"Yeah, I could see that, a surprise visit. Meet the employees—that sort of thing. Like the town meeting stuff, only I won't have to answer any questions. I need more of that. All of this Washington publicity is dragging down my numbers, and it's only been nine months. We are playing right into Limbaugh's hand. I really wish we could figure out a way to bring him down. The best Emanuel has come up with is planting a story that he's back on the horse."

"So, you want me to go ahead with this? I can have my staff start looking for a bank. We can get hold of the Chicago office and consult with them. We've a guy there that seems to be having a lot of success working with small banks."

The president's desk hummed again. "Yes."

Mumble, mumble.

"Okay. Send them in, in five minutes." A frown crossed the president's face. "Dodd and Frank are here. It's like Abbott and Costello, and they still can't figure out who's on first. Okay, we good here? You are going to set this up? What's our time frame?"

"I'll have to get back to you once I get a handle on a location."

The president stood, signaling the end of the meeting. "Don't take too long. I need some positive press."

Yusef Olajuwon

Chapter 24

The Sox were in town for their last home stand of the season, drawing a less than enthusiastic crowd since they were in last place with no hope of redemption. Jasmine Jackson sat between Terry Myers and Yusuf Olajuwon, bored with the baseball game, playing a hand-held video game and listening to Fifty Cent rap through her iPod ear buds. Office calls were being routed through her cell phone into her iPod, but there had been only two calls all afternoon, and they were of no significance.

The rap cut out intermittently, signaling a call coming in on the cell, and she answered, "Department of the Treasury, Midwest Regional Office, Jasmine speaking. How may I help you?"

"This is Secretary Geithner. Is Mr. Olajuwon in?"

"And what company are you with?"

Geithner hesitated and then said, "There seems to be a lot of background noise. What did you say?"

FIRST STATE BANK and (dis)TRUST of Hinkley County

Ricardo Rodriques pulled a sharp liner to the left field wall for a solid double, and the crowd erupted, happy for some excitement and a reason to stand up and stretch.

Jasmine cupped her hand around the phone, trying to insulate it from the crowd noise. "I'm sorry; there is a lot of static on the line. What did you say your name is?"

"This is Timothy Geithner, Treasury Secretary of the United States. Who are you, and why is there so much yelling in the background? Is there some problem?"

Jasmine sensed it might be an important call, even though she still wasn't sure who was calling. "Mr. Olajuwon is not taking calls right now. He's in conference. Can I take your number and have him return your call?"

Olajuwon sat down, forcing his large torso into the box seat. "Who is it, babe? Tell 'em to call back. You're missing the best part of the game."

Jasmine put her hand over the phone. "It's somebody's secretary. Wants to talk to you."

The next batter hit a long fly ball into the right field corner, causing the outfielder to sprint for the catch. "Look at that white boy run," Yusuf said, smiling. "Take a number, babe. I can't talk right now."

Geithner was yelling into the phone as Jasmine brought it back to her ear. "What's going on there? Hello, hello."

Jasmine thought for a second and then said in her best monotone, "I'm sorry. This call cannot be completed as dialed. Please hang up and try again." She hung up the phone.

Mack the Dog

Chapter 25

Murt Featherstone sat at her desk eating a pickled tongue sandwich that she had packed in wax paper that morning along with some garden radishes and her favorite side dish—pickled jalapeño peppers she had canned the fall before. The picnic was spread across her desk, and her phone was off the hook, signaling her lunch hour had begun. The sign on her office door read *BACK AT 1:00,* even though she was fully visible from the hall.

A medium-height balding man dressed in a blue pinstriped suit with an Ivy League-trademark striped tie stood at the door holding his briefcase and examining the sign. He looked at Murt and frowned, thought the problem through, and tried the door to see if it was locked. The door opened freely, and the man stuck his head in and gave a pursed smile.

"Can't read, huh?" Murt remarked, taking another gulp of her tongue sandwich. "Man dressed like you; yud think he could read."

"Uh, I did see the sign, but I thought maybe it was intended for someone other than you."

FIRST STATE BANK and (dis)TRUST of Hinkley County

Murt picked at her teeth with her fingernail, trying to dislodge some of the stringy meat. "Ain't no mistake. It's lunch time." She looked at the clock on the wall. "For another twenty minutes."

"Is there anyone else that can help me?"

Murt held the sandwich in front of her face, preparing for another bite, then slowly looked around the silent office before looking back at the bald head sticking through the door. "Look like there is anyone else here to you?"

Murt shook her head, sighed, set her sandwich down, slowly got up, fumbled around in her purse, which was hanging over the back of her chair, walked around the office counter, and over to the door.

The man started to enter, assuming Murt was offering to interrupt her lunch.

Instead, Murt gave him a shove, pushed the door shut, and locked it. Without looking at the man staring through the glass door, she returned to her desk, put the keys back in her purse, sat down, and resumed her lunch.

Promptly at one o'clock, Murt disposed of her lunch remains, stretched, put the phone back on the receiver, extricated herself from her chair, and slowly walked over to the office door. The man was still standing outside. She unlocked the door, removed the sign, and returned to her desk.

The man opened the door and this time, with caution, made a complete entrance, and stood at the front counter.

Murt looked up and then looked back down at the crossword puzzle book she had opened for her afternoon amusement and said, "Somethin' I can do for you?"

The man assumed an authoritative stance, placing his briefcase on the counter with his hands folded and resting there as well. "My request is a simple one. I am interested in any recent transactions of large land purchases or mortgages on same. More specifically, those involving the name Quince or any company affiliated with the name."

Murt looked up at the man and said, "And who might you be?"

"I was not aware that it was necessary to present identification to access public records."

"I'd say you was right. But then, I'd say it ain't necessary for me to help you, neither. There's a whole room full of records back there, and there's a whole basement full of more down stairs. Have at it." Murt looked back down at her crossword puzzle.

There was silence for a long moment, and then the man said, "I'm John Westmorland, attorney for the Midwest Development Corporation. We are doing some work for a client, and we are interested in the transactions I spoke of. Can you assist me? I would be most appreciative."

Murt looked back up and sighed. "There ain't been any large land transfers recorded in over a year, except a farm or two that have been transferred within families. Now, this Quince fellow you referred to, he's been sniffin' around town. He took an option on the Thornberry place, but it ain't been recorded. Don't have to record an option. The option is for twenty some acres next to the interchange south of town. You know where I mean? You probably drove right by it when you came in on Main Street. Says he's gonna build an amusement park or something. Good lookin' feller. We went round a time or two." Murt smiled for the first time.

Westmorland smiled back, noting a piece of radish stuck to Murt's front tooth. "Sounds like a pretty firm deal, then. Did he tell you how much the option was for?"

"I said we went round a time or two. I didn't say we reviewed his bank account."

"Does this Thornberry have a realtor or an attorney that he's dealing through?"

"You'd have to ask him."

Westmorland squinted at the name displayed on Murt's desk. "Well, Miss Featherstone, you have been very helpful. One other thing, I assume the county commissioners have offices in this building. Are they normally available for an audience?"

"My brother's a county commissioner. He usually comes to the courthouse after he gets his chores done. That's Sid Featherstone, but I suspect he's gone by now. Chet Sadinski does about the same thing, then he goes to lunch, but it's hard to tell where you might find him now. Ralph Bellows is the other commissioner. He's probably drunk by now, so it won't do you no good to talk to him. Their regular monthly meetin' is next Tuesday. That's probably the best time to catch 'em. You could go upstairs and talk to Mable Hinkley. She's the commissioners' secretary. You got to talk loud, though. She's hard a-hearin'."

Westmorland started to suffer from information overload and pulled his briefcase from the counter. "Thanks again, Miss Featherstone. You say if I just head out of town the way I came in, I'll pass the Thornberry property?"

"It's the big white house next to the highway interchange. Can't miss it."

Westmorland sat in his Lincoln reporting his findings to Olajuwon.

"Quince seems to be on the move. He's taken an option on some property just on the outskirts of town."

"How much?" Olajuwon demanded.

"She didn't know. I drove by the location, but there was a big dog sitting in the driveway, and there didn't appear to be anyone home. I'm still trying to track down whether the owner has representation. There's no realtor sign or anything I can see."

"Find out. What about the background on Quince? Anything new?"

"My investigator says everything is legit. His background is vague, but there are no red flags."

"Washington wants me to push this deal so they can use it as an example of the benefit the T.A.R.P. program means to Middle America. They want small town appeal. I tried to move them in another direction, but it's the only deal that fit. We will just have to be careful, make sure Quince understands the need for confidentiality when it comes to the fees."

Westmorland chuckled. "You say they want small town? Believe me; they'll get a lot of that. You should get a load of the gal that works in the recorder's office. She wears her hair in this big curl on top of her forehead. It looks like something out of a Betty Boop cartoon. And then she said she had a thing going with Quince. I hope his taste for decorating whatever he plans on building is better than his taste for women."

Olajuwon went on as if he didn't hear the comment. "Myers talked to Quince and threw the bait in front of him. Sounded like he's hooked. I talked to the bank president this morning and Quince hasn't been in to see him about financing other than to throw around the idea, and the bank guy is still playing hardball. I can handle that. Their board meeting is scheduled for next Tuesday, so I want Quince wrapped by then. I need to get back to Geithner's people so they can start the P.R. with teases leading up to the big play. Go back to the farm or whatever and get as much as you can. I need to be prepared for this board meeting so we can approve a loan. Remember, we're looking at over a million."

Westmorland slowly approached Thornberry's driveway, a long lane leading to an open yard with numerous shade trees. The house faced the road with the four-lane highway some distance behind it. There was a barn that had not seen paint in several decades, an implement shed in similar condition, and a garage whose swinging doors were only half-closed, apparently unable to ingest the rear bumper and taillights of an old car stored within. The house showed signs of wear, but the metal roof appeared stout, and the porch, though sloping at an odd stance, also appeared stable. It was adorned with a rocker and a wooden swing suspended by chains from the ceiling.

About fifty yards from the front porch lay a big dog with long, dark, matted hair. Westmorland couldn't help but think, *He has a pet wolf.*

He turned into the lane and approached the yard, stopping a good twenty yards from the dog. He was close enough to note that the dog was not tied. Feeling no need to test its attitude, he gave a long blast of his horn. To his amazement, the dog didn't even flinch.

There was no movement at the house, and the dog simply lay still, staring at him. He put the car back in gear, and with the slightest of movements, started toward the dog. The dog lay in the middle of the lane, just where the yard gave way to wheat stubble. There was no room to drive around the dog without going into a small ditch, so he took the initiative to approach it, assuming it would eventually move or become Lincoln grill meat. That plan failed miserably. The dog did not move.

When the dog disappeared from view in front of the car, Westmorland stopped. He rolled the window down and was about to yell at the dog when he heard a low gurgling grow. He moved his face closer to the window, trying to peek over the door to see if the dog had walked around the car.

"Nice doggy, good dog," he said cautiously as he peeked over the half-open window.

Without warning, the huge dog lunged onto the hood of the car, teeth bared, pushing his snout against the windshield, and making a fearsome sound as he snapped his huge teeth.

Westmoreland pushed himself against the back of the seat, as far from the windshield as he could get, struck with fear. He threw the car into reverse and shoved the accelerator to the floor. The wheels spun, and the car jumped backwards, throwing the dog off the hood, but Westmorland, concentrating on the fate of the vicious dog, ended up in the ditch along the lane only a few yards from where he started. The soggy earth absorbed his spinning rear tires, and his escape was halted as fast as it started. He shoved the car in and out of gear, trying to rock out of the hole with no success. Giving up, he pressed the up button, and the window closed just in time to avoid the wrath of the rabid acting dog as it bounded around the car and jumped against the closed window, gnawing at the door handle.

Westmorland weighed his options. He could call nine-one-one, assuming this isolated county had such a service, and hope for assistance. He could call a tow service on his cell and let the tow guy deal with the dog. He envisioned a three-hundred-pound tow truck driver with a big gun. Or he could wait until the dog tired of the standoff and went to the house for dinner then make a run for it.

Concentrating on the snarling dog he did not notice Thornberry walk off his porch and down the lane to the disabled car. The dog stopped snapping and growling, and Westmorland peeked over the edge of the driver's door to see if he had wandered off or was playing possum, waiting for the chance to attack when he stepped out of the car.

"You tried to run over my dog. It pissed him off." Thornberry said as he stooped down and looked in the passenger window at Westmorland.

A push of the button lowered the passenger door window. "Where is he? Keep that dog away from me."

"Pretty damn demanding for somebody that's up to his ass in mud on private property, wouldn't you say?"

"You can't let a vicious dog like that run around. You could get sued, you know."

Thornberry smiled, his tobacco-stained teeth showing through his three-day beard stubble. "Suppose I could, but he usually don't let nobody get away once he gets a-holt of 'em, so there ain't much left for anybody to sue about."

"I can't just sit in this car all day. I need a tow truck or something."

"I suppose something could be arranged. There's a big John Deere in that barn over yonder that could probably pick this here car up and throw it, if it had a mind to, but before we go to that trouble, ol' Mack and me would like to know what you are doing out here. He's just a sittin' where he likes to sit, and you try to run over him. Then you talk about suin' us."

Westmorland looked out the passenger window and saw Mack sitting next to Thornberry. He appeared to be smiling, or at least smirking, his lips raised just enough to show his long canines.

"I stopped to talk to you. There's a rumor around town that you sold out to a fellow who is building some kind of amusement park or something. I don't see any for sale sign in your yard or anything. I was just wondering if it was true."

"And what business would it be of your'n?"

Westmorland peeked over the door again, and Mack continued to smirk, his canines dripping slobber. He pondered the question and said, "I work for a firm handling some of the financing, and we are just confirming that the principal is moving along as he says he is. You can't be too careful these days. Somebody's always trying to pull something."

"So, what you're tellin' me is it ain't none of your business what I'm doin', which is what I thought when I walked out here. You want to know what that feller is doin', the one you call your principal, you better ask him." Thornberry looked down at Mack. "You stay here and don't let him out of the car whilst I go get the Deere and some chains."

Westmorland looked over the door again as Thornberry walked toward the barn. Mack, smirk still in place, winked at him; at least, it looked that way.

Yusef Olajuwon

Chapter 26

Yusuf Olajuwon, Jasmine Jackson, and three level-one account clerks sat at one end of the conference table. Sook Kim Chow, a treasury department official, sat at the other end, each studying the others as they waited for a conference call to connect on the telephone in the middle of the table.

Jasmine adjusted her blouse, allowing her cleavage to offer the best possible presentation after noting Chow's inadvertent glance in her direction. She broke the silence and asked, "Sooky, hon, you want me to get some water? We have some of that new flavored stuff."

Chow smiled at the intimate way Jasmine addressed him after just being introduced. "Thank you for asking, but I think our call will be coming through any minute. Maybe after our meeting—I mean, if you have time—"

The phone beeped and a computer voice said, "A party has joined your call."

"Hello? Uh, hello. This is Secretary Geithner. Anyone there?"

Chow jumped to his feet and stood erect, much to the other participants' surprise. Staring straight ahead with his chin up and his hands pressed to his sides, he responded loudly, "Yes, sir, Mr. Secretary. Chow here for the department. We are joined by Yusuf Olajuwon," Chow relaxed for an instant and smiled at Jasmine and then continued, "Jasmine Jackson, and three subordinates. We are ready for your instructions." Chow sat down but kept his body rigid, pen erect, ready to take notes.

"Uh, okay. I don't know that I am here to give instructions, but I would like to know what progress has been made. Mr. Olajuwon, are we still on track with the community bank we discussed? We are currently looking at early October for our publicity event. We want to be just ahead of local and state elections. Will you be ready?"

"Yes, suh," Yusuf responded loudly and with some sarcasm, mocking Chow, then tempered his answer by continuing, "we are progressing with the bank and the investor and should be able to present a perfect picture of government and private enterprise working in harmony." He winked at Jasmine. She covered her smile with her hand, holding back laughter.

There was silence on the line, as if Geithner was absorbing the response. "Okay, then. That leaves us less than thirty days to wrap this entire project up. This is confidential. There are to be no leaks. Do I make myself clear?"

There were "yes, sirs" all around the room.

"If this project gets any advance press, I will know exactly where it came from. Chow?"

"Yes, sir," Chow almost screamed.

"You will be responsible—I mean, you will be held responsible if there are any problems. Do you understand?"

"Yes, sir."

"I am producing a memo as we speak to Emanuel advising him to proceed with the logistics. I am putting my name on this memo, so if anything goes wrong, the president is going to be asking me about it. Do you understand?"

"Yes, sir." With each response, Chow grew louder, causing feedback in the phone monitor.

"Are there any questions?"

Jasmine cleared her throat. "Ah, uh, do it mean that I, we get to meet the president?"

Chow's rigid stance suddenly went limp as he shook his head in disbelief.

"I don't— Who is asking the question?"

"My name is Jasmine Jackson. I'm the assistant to the assistant undersecretary." Jasmine looked around the room at everyone staring at her. "Suh."

There was a few seconds of static-filled silence and then, "Well, that might be arranged. I don't know how this event will be planned just yet, and the president sometimes goes his own way, so we will just have to see. Anything else?"

Chow regained his composure and stood up, re-assuming his military stance. "I think not, Mr. Secretary. You can count on me—uh, the entire office—to give one hundred percent toward this effort. Signing off."

The static continued. "Well, okay. Yeah, signing, uh, off, I guess." There was a beep, and Geithner was gone.

Chow sat back down. "Okay, you heard our orders. Now we have to get to work. There is a lot to be done in the next two weeks."

Olajuwon stared across the table at Chow. "What the fuck you talkin' about? Orders? This ain't no military operation."

"You heard the Secretary. I'm in charge of this operation, and we are going to cover every possibility of failure. That's the key to success—know what mistakes can be made and take decisive action before they happen."

Olajuwon got up, and Jasmine stood as well. They turned and walked toward the door, and Olajuwon said as they left the room, "Babe, you hear that bullshit? Yes, sir. No sir. Like he's in the fucking army or something."

CHAPTER 27

Marge Stopher sat at the dispatch desk in the Hinkley County Sheriff's office putting peanut butter on a large chunk of chocolate she had broken off a bar that came from the vending machine. Once that maneuver was completed, she carefully peeled a banana, and with her Swiss army knife cut a large cross section and placed it on top of the peanut butter. She smiled, admiring her work, and without hesitation, stuffed the whole thing in her mouth and chomped with complete satisfaction.

The phone rang and she hesitated, trying to chew and swallow as fast as she could, but the peanut butter, an extra large glob, was stuck to the top of her mouth.

The phone rang for the fourth time.

"Himpky theriff afith."

There was silence on the line and then a voice inquired, "Uh, is this the Hinkley County Sheriff's office?"

"Yeth, it ith. Pleath hold." Marge jumped up and ran to the water fountain in the hall outside her office. Swallowing, almost choking, she chewed with voracity, not wanting to spit the sumptuous morsel out after all the work putting it together. Once she had cleared her mouth, she returned to the phone.

"Sorry, had another call, an emergency. Is this an emergency?"

"No, I would like to speak to Sheriff Miner."

"And who is calling?" Marge asked, gaining authority with a clear sounding voice.

"This is Colonel Sam Wyeth, special security detail out of Fort Campbell Air Force base. Is the sheriff in?"

"He is not in. Out on a call or something. What you need him for?" Marge cradled the phone in the crook of her neck and started preparing another peanut butter delight.

"I need to talk to the sheriff personally. When will he be back? Can you patch me through?"

"I can call him on his cell. Don't mean he'll answer."

"Oh, well, just give me the number. I need to talk to him."

Marge laughed aloud. "Yeah, right. I'm going to give out the sheriff's personal cell number. After I do that, I'll go down to the unemployment office and get in line. Why don't you give me your personal cell number, and when I find the sheriff, I'll have him call you?"

Wyeth hesitated. "Sorry, you are not authorized to have that information."

"Now you know how the sheriff feels." Marge placed the sliced banana on top of the peanut butter.

"Madam, this is a matter of national security, and I do not have time to discuss the reasoning behind our precautions. Just give me the number."

Marge stopped her sandwich assembly, sighed into the receiver, and said, "For somebody in the military, assuming you are who you say you are, you don't listen worth a damn. I don't give numbers out over the phone, no matter who calls. Now you want to leave your number or not? It don't matter to me."

Wyeth contemplated the situation and realized his position and power were pretty insignificant while talking to a civilian. "Okay, have him call my office as soon as you locate him. This is very important and time sensitive." Wyeth gave his number and hung up.

Marge admired her work and ate it with one bite.

Sheriff Miner called in when he finished with his haircut while waiting for his mobile sheriff's office S.U.V. to be hand washed at Floyd's Auto Detail behind the Super Value.

"Marge, what's the name of that guy that painted your barn doors, the one that did that fancy squiggly stuff? Floyd here says he wants to paint a sign on the front of this old garage. Thought that guy would be perfect." Miner leaned against another parked car watching two Latino kids wash his truck.

Marge hesitated, trying to remember the name, and responded, "I can't remember. I'll have to ask Harold when I get home. It's his second cousin on his mother's side. The kid has some kind of art degree from that school over in the Falls. You have to keep an eye on him; he likes to snoop around when you're not lookin'. I think we lost a couple dollars out of the cookie jar, if you know what I mean."

Miner pulled the phone from his ear. "Hey, wipe that back window again; it's got streaks all over it. Como sta?" He put the phone back to his ear. "What's Mexican for 'understand'? Just because Floyd does this as a favor so I don't bust him for hiring illegals, they think they can just do a half-ass job. You gonna find out the name? Can you call Harold before I leave?"

"He's out cleaning the ditch next to the driveway. Can't reach him until supper tonight. Uh, some military guy called from Campbell. Sez he needs to talk to you right away. Kind of a jerk, but I guess they're all that way."

"What did he want?"

"Jeez, Sheriff, you think he's gonna talk to me? You're lucky he let me take a message. Otherwise, he'd still be on hold. Said it was some kind of military secret. No, he said it had something to do with national security."

"That's what they always say. He probably wants to bring a bunch of recruits over to the state park for another camp thing. They're like boy scouts, only they never clean the place up after they leave. They always want me to make all the arrangements and seal the whole park off, for national security reasons, of course."

"Well, you want his number, or wait until you get back?"

"He'll call back. They always do."

Miner walked through the rear door of the courthouse and into the sheriff's office, hanging his Stetson on the hat rack and checking the dispatch log for any recent calls. Marge wasn't at the dispatch terminal, and he noted a line was on hold.

Marge came through the door and said, "He's waiting for you."

"Who?"

"The guy from Campbell. He's been on hold for about twenty minutes. He called again right after you called the last time. Said he would wait."

"He'll have to keep waiting. I have to use the head." Miner picked up the *Hinkley Messenger,* walked back out in the hall, and disappeared.

Returning a few minutes later, Miner asked, "He still there?"

"Far as I know."

Miner went into his office, checked the numerous papers on his desk as he got comfortable, reached back to the portable refrigerator built into the credenza, pulled out a bottled water, and then lifted the receiver and took his call.

"Sheriff Miner here."

There was a silence punctuated only by an occasional heavy breath. "I've been waiting for over thirty minutes."

"Really? Marge said it was only twenty, but then she doesn't wear a watch."

"It's thirty minutes I could have been accomplishing something of importance, rather than sitting here with this phone stuck in my ear waiting for you."

"Well, now that you got that off your chest, what is it you want?"

"As much as I hate to say it, I need your department's assistance. What I am about to tell you needs kept in complete confidence. No one in your office or in your county should be informed until the last minute, when I give the command."

"How's this sound? Don't tell me until you, what did you say, give the command or push the button or whatever? That way, you don't have to worry about it."

"Believe me, if I could handle it that way, I would, but I have orders to bring you into the mix and keep you informed. We have received a preliminary itinerary for the president, which includes Hinkley County. He is planning a trip to meet officials of a local bank. It will be publicized as a spontaneous stop between scheduled meetings in Chicago and Los Angeles. Right now, the choreography calls for him to be choppered down from O'Hare. The current date is October five at thirteen hundred hours. All of that could change and probably will.

"I will be doing the preliminary recon Thursday—myself and two secret service agents. You can accompany us and answer questions. We will be there at oh-eight-hundred. Any questions?"

"What if I don't want to accompany you?"

"Miner, why do you always have to be such an asshole? It's the president of the United States, you jack-off. He's coming to your town. You are probably going to be on national TV."

"Yeah, I hadn't thought of that. Okay, I'll drive you around. Where do you want to start?"

"You aren't going to drive us around. We will be in an unmarked. Remember, this is confidential. There can't be any advance publicity. The whole idea is for this to be spontaneous. He comes in and there are some photo ops. His correspondent entourage shoots some action for the evening news, they do their stand-ups in front of the bank or whatever, and that's it. He gets back in the chopper and is gone. The biggest disruption will be the day before and the morning of when the Secret Service brings in the bomb dogs and they set up their

FIRST STATE BANK and **(dis)**TRUST of Hinkley County

security perimeter. That's where your department will have to keep things in line."

Miner's attitude abruptly changed as he envisioned the photo ops. "We can handle that."

"Okay, I'll have a lot more for you Thursday. Remember; do not share this information with anyone, understood?"

Miner walked into the outer office where Marge sat at the dispatch desk. "You are not going to believe this, Marge."

Ralph Bellows

Chapter 28

J.R. sat at the conference table in the meeting room of the Hinkley Country Club studying notes he had prepared for the board meeting. The balance of the board members, with the exception of Ralph Bellows, stood in the corner of the room surrounding Yusuf Olajuwon, interrogating him about the amusement park project and its impact on the county.

Father Tom, his voice filled with excitement, said, "I've been thinking. There are going to be a lot of people spending weekends, and they are not going to have access to a chapel. If I could talk to this Quince guy—it would be good to have a non-denominational chapel in the park. I've talked to Monsignor Skinner, and he said he would talk to Cardinal Joseph about bringing in one of the Sisters of Perpetual Harmony to help as support staff. I could talk to the Council of Ministers and see if the other denominations want to participate. Of course, the Central State Catholic Diocese would have to be the primary—"

Fred Chin Lee interrupted, "Come on, Tom. You think he is going to build a cathedral next to the tilt-a-whirl? Maybe you can get him to put in a bingo room, if you agree to split the profit fifty-fifty." This drew a chuckle from the others.

Lee's tone grew serious. "I was thinking about the dry cleaning concession, though. You know, the hotel is going to have to have laundry service and dry cleaning available to the guests. I need to talk to this Quince. You know when he'll be back in town?"

Sid Johnson, owner of Sid's Contracting, spoke up, trying to get his pitch in. "Yusuf, does this qualify for one of those spade or shovel-ready things they are talking about? I mean, we could start building roads and parking lots tomorrow. The state will probably have to re-do the interchange to accommodate the traffic. Can't you get them to throw in a couple million right now to get this started?"

Olajuwon just smiled. He had everyone on his side even before the meeting started.

J.R. looked up, sighed, rubbed his forehead, and said, "Okay, everyone, sit down and let's get started. Bellows is probably—"

Ralph Bellows burst into the room, drink in hand, bending over and panting as if he had just finished a mile run.

J.R. gave Ralph a disgusted look and started to call the meeting to order again after the disruption.

Ralph held up his hand, shaking it as he gasped for breath.

"What, Ralph? Just sit down so we can get started," J.R. said, looking back down at his notes.

"Wait, wait," Ralph spit out, still trying to gain composure while he took a long draw on his cocktail. "I just talked to Harry Stopher—you know, Marge's husband." Ralph again bent over and pulled in a deep breath. "You guys are not going to believe this, and it can't go beyond this room. I'm serious."

The rest of the board members started taking their seats, with Olajuwon sitting at the far end of the table, away from J.R. As usual, they paid no attention to Ralph.

J.R. again addressed Bellows. "Sit down, Ralph. We can hear your gossip after the meeting. We have some important issues to get settled."

Bellows straightened and firmly said, "Is that right? Well, is it more important than meeting the president of the United States?"

The room quieted.

"What in the world are you talking about?" J.R. asked. "The commissioners figured out a way to get a free trip to Washington?"

There was a chuckle from the other board members.

"Not quite," Ralph said indignantly. "Like I said, this information is confidential, but Marge said the sheriff got a call from the Secret Service. The president is planning a trip, and he's going to stop here."

J.R. shook his head and said, "Ralph, think about it. Why would the president want to come here? How would he get here? By bus?" J.R. again shook his head. "Can we get started now?"

"I'm telling you that's what she said. Other people have said the same thing. I think it has something to do with this amusement park thing—you know, a big construction project in a little community like this."

Olajuwon had been silent, listening to the guesses and questionable facts. Finally, he said, "Uh, there may be some truth to what Mr. Bellows is saying."

Heads turned toward Olajuwon, and J.R. stared in disbelief.

"I have been in contact with the president's travel office and his spokesperson. It is true; there is a preliminary plan to bring the president here for an informal meeting with community leaders, emphasizing the success of the T.A.R.P. program. But—" Olajuwon hesitated for a dramatic pause, drawing emphasis to his next statement. "This is all contingent on the decisions made here, tonight, by this board."

Everyone stared at Olajuwon, absorbing his indictment of their importance.

Bellows could not help himself, and turned to J.R. and remarked, "Gossip, huh? Doesn't sound like gossip to me."

J.R. cleared his throat and said without much authority, "Uh-hum, okay, but what does this group have to do with this, this visit, or whatever it's being called?"

"This whole project depends on the financing—on this bank and this board to approve the financing. Now—" Olajuwon had a large pile of collated and stapled booklets in front of him, and he rose and distributed them to each member of the board while he continued. "This is a complete finance portfolio put together by a firm that specializes in packaging projects like this. It is complete regarding the basic plan and initial monetary requirements. We are looking at an approximate ten-million-dollar project that includes a hotel and surrounding infrastructure. I know this is too much for you to digest while we sit here, but we really don't have time to delay a decision, at least a decision to move forward."

J.R. interrupted, "We can't just approve a loan for ten million dollars based on a bunch of papers. Are y-y-you nuts?"

"Calm down, Mr. Roberts. It's not as if you are writing a check tonight. The board just needs to approve the spirit of the project. The only funds that may be dispersed in the first thirty to ninety days are the fees and cost of the environmental impact study—phase one, two, and maybe three, if necessary."

Sid Johnson spoke as he leafed through the booklet. "Wow, this is really detailed. J.R., did you see this picture—conceptual drawing—of the hotel in here? I'm impressed. To tell you the truth, up to this point, I had my doubts. I mean, you want to believe something like this could happen, but you know—and now it's all contingent on us loaning the money."

"And it's not even our money at risk; it's government money," Father Tom inserted with enthusiasm.

J.R. gathered his thoughts and tried to bring the group back under control. "Whoa, whoa, slow down. Didn't you hear what I said? We are still a bank. We still have to act as if we know what we are doing. There are procedures, and one of them is to look at this type of project with reservation and some common sense. Our bank has never made a loan over two million dollars. Do you know why? Because it's risky. We let the big banks take those risks because when this cowboy decides to take off with the money, we won't be holding the bag."

Yusuf spoke up. "Ah, but J.R., if you look at—" Yusuf pawed through the booklet until he found the right page. "Look at page fifty-seven, subset number three A. You will see that eighty percent of the loan is insured by the small business administration through their economic stabilization loan guarantee program. The most your bank can be liable for is two million, and you have almost made that much off the T.A.R.P. funds already."

All of the heads in the room turned toward J.R., who was still trying to find the section of the booklet with the guarantee. He looked up and saw that everyone was expecting him to respond. "Well, uh, we just can't commit to something like this on the spur of the moment. I haven't even talked to this Quince character, other than to have him strut around the office and act as if he was some kind of movie star or something. I don't like it." He looked back down at the booklet.

Fred Chin Lee took the lead. "Well, I agree with Mister Olajuwon. I think we owe it to this community to get involved. I vote that we approve the loan."

"Y-y-you w-w-what? Y-you c-c-can't vote. There's n-n-nothing t-to vote on." J.R. rubbed his forehead, trying to calm himself.

Sid Johnson stood and said, "I second that vote."

Father Tom said, "I third it. Is that right? I mean, I agree with Fred and Sid."

"Shut up! S-s-shut up," J.R. yelled. He stood and started shoving papers into his briefcase as if it was an overstuffed wastebasket. "Th-th-this m-m-meeting is over."

Ralph Bellows swallowed the last of his drink and stood. "I wonder what kind of scotch the president drinks. I need a re-fill."

Olajuwon stood, carefully arranging his papers. "Well, we've had a very productive meeting tonight. I believe this project will be right on schedule and all of you will be proud of what you have done tonight."

FIRST STATE BANK and (dis)TRUST of Hinkley County

J.R.'s face was red and his hands were shaking. "N-n-nothing h-has been done. D-do you h-h-hear m-m-me?"

Olajuwon slapped Fred Chin Lee on the back as they left the room. "Let's go down to the locker room bar, and I'll fill you in on the president's visit—how these things usually go."

Chapter 29

"J.R., I only have a few minutes. I realize this is an emergency, but I have other patients. They all have needs. What is it? Maybe your family doctor could help?" Doctor Rubinski's laptop rested on his knees while he sat on the overstuffed leather chair, his reading glasses propped low on his nose as he tapped the keys.

J.R. sat on the edge of the couch, twisting his hands as if he was wringing out a washcloth, his vacant stare unfocused. "I-I c-c-can't s-s-s-stop st-st-stuttering." He sighed, happy to have gotten the sentence out.

Rubinski looked up and said, "What happened?"

"W-w-what? N-n-nothing. I-I-I j-j-ju— Oh, f-forget it."

"Something has you in a state of—well, it's like shock, but not exactly. Did the girl end your relationship? Cut you off?" Rubinski tapped a few more keys.

"Is t-t-that all y-you s-s-shrinks c-c-can think about? M-my s-sex life? Freud. Ev, everything i-is F-f-f—Sigmund."

"Okay, if it isn't the girl or a relationship, what is it? The only way you are going to overcome this is to face the issue that has you so upset. Is it the bank? That's the other issue you spoke of."

J.R. increased his hand wringing.

"Okay, something happened at the bank. J.R., I'm not making any accusations or anything, so just bear with me here, but is the bank in trouble? Have you done something that you fear will be discovered?"

"N-n-no I-I-I—" J.R. raised one hand and shook it, signaling he could not get it out.

"Okay, here's what I want you to do. Sometimes this works, sometimes it doesn't, but it does offer a transitional remedy to help you overcome this disability, at least temporarily. I want you to think of a song, a melody you are familiar with. It can be anything—*Jingle Bells* or the happy birthday melody. Everyone knows those. Seriously, J.R., do you have a melody in mind?"

J.R. looked dumbfounded, but after a moment of contemplation, he gave an affirmative nod.

"Okay, each time you start to say something, think of that melody and incorporate your thought into that melody." Rubinski thought for a second and then said in a melodic way, using the melody from *Jingle Bells*, "Okay, here we go. Okay here we go. I'm talking using the *Jingle Bells* tune all the way. It will help you lose the stutter, and eventually you'll forget the tune. Now you try it."

J.R. stared for a few seconds, rubbed his forehead, opened his mouth, hesitated, then started, "O-o-okay, okay. I'm using a tune. I'm using the tune all the way. Over the hills a-and through the snow, I'm using the tune all the way. Th-the—wait." He thought for a second and started the melody over again. "The only problem is, the only problem is, I don't know enough of the song all the way."

"Good," Rubinski said. "I think this is going to work. We are going to have to end for now. I have people waiting. Try the singsong remedy for right now, and I think in a short time, you won't have to think about it. The stutter will go away. If it reoccurs, you can always bring the melody back and start over."

❖

J.R. walked through the bank lobby past Sally without acknowledging her or anyone else. His office door was open, and as he approached, he saw the Stetson laying next to the chair and the top of Quince's head. He stopped and made an abrupt turn, looking at Sally. She shrugged her shoulders and turned back to her empty desk.

Bit turned and stretched out his hand for a shake. "How we doin' today, J.R.? Sorry I couldn't call ahead, but things are really movin' along. Thought we better talk."

J.R. didn't shake the outstretched hand. He went straight to his desk and sat down. The two stared at each other. Bit smiled, waiting for J.R. to respond. J.R. tried to decide what to do and how to sing something.

Finally, J.R. had no choice but to respond. "P-pl—" He thought of *Jingle Bells*. "Please, close the door; please, close the door. Please, close the door all the way."

Bit's smile faded as he stared at J.R. Then he looked at the open door, shrugged, and got up and closed it. "Something wrong there, J.R.? You look a little tense."

"I really don't have time. I really don't have time. Can't we do this some other time all the way?"

Bit stared at J.R. intently, trying to figure out what was going on. His first thought was that this was some kind of joke, but J.R. was not the joking kind. "Well, J.R., looks like we are going to be doin' some business. I understand your board meetin' last night went well. Got everything approved. That was quite a presentation, wasn't it? It impressed the hell out of me, how about you?"

J.R.'s face turned red, but he remained silent.

"Cat got your tongue, or are you just so excited about this project and all the doin's that you don't know what to say?"

J.R. looked like he was going to burst as he stood and placed his palms on the desk. "I'm telling you, I'm telling you,

FIRST STATE BANK and (dis)TRUST of Hinkley County

there is no loan deal all the way. Over the hills and through the snow, this is all going away."

Bit lost his smile and tipped his head back in complete confusion. "J.R., this whole thing's got you in a dither." Bit stood and rubbed his chin in thought and then said, "We need to talk. Come with me out to the parking lot, where we can have some privacy."

Chapter 30

Sheriff Miner was sitting in his office reading the State Sheriff Association's monthly newsletter when Marge yelled from the outer office, "They're here. Just called and said they are waiting in the parking lot."

Miner took his time, finished his coffee, walked over to the coffee machine and wiped out his cup, checked the call log, retrieved his hat from the hat rack, straightened his shirt and belt, and walked out of the office heading for the parking lot. Outside the courthouse exit sat a large black SUV with heavily tinted windows, two antennas, and government plates.

Miner walked up and opened a back door. Wyeth and two other men sat in the vehicle, all three wearing dark aviator sunglasses and black suits.

"Wasn't sure this was the right car, unmarked like it is and all. I'm sure we'll be inconspicuous driving around town in this. People'll be looking for the black helicopters next."

"That's enough, Miner. It was the only vehicle at the motor pool that we could all fit in. This is Special Agent Stokes and Special Agent Carter. They are secret service, special presidential security detail. They will be doing the initial recon and will bring in the logistics people—probably next week. They will give you direction on what part your people will play. Today, we need you to give us directions so we can set up the initial route and security placement. Special Agent Stokes, where do you want to start?"

Stokes sat in the front seat looking out the window, showing no reaction to Wyeth's remarks or the question directed at him. After a moment of silence he said without turning his head, "Let's look at the bank. From there we need to look at all of the buildings between the highway interchange and the bank. Carter will photograph the buildings. We need to see the rear of the buildings as well."

Miner interrupted, "So, is he coming in from the highway in a motorcade? We kind of wondered since we don't have an airport—a paved airport, anyway."

No one answered.

"What? That's a secret?" Miner asked with a smirk.

Wyeth responded, "Right now, everything is on a need to know basis. Right now, you don't need to know."

"Really?" Miner said, crossing his arms with his hat in his lap. "The way I see it, you need me more than I need you, so why don't you take this undercover bat mobile and find your own way around town." Miner reached for the door handle and started to get out.

Wyeth put the truck back in park and turned with his arm over the seat. "Okay, Miner, you made your point. Get back in here. Right now, nothing is certain. He could come in by helicopter, or he may land in Cougar Falls and motorcade. We don't know. Satisfied?"

Miner pulled his legs back into the vehicle and closed the door. "The bank's just down the street, on Main Street, like everything else in this town."

Ralphy and Witherspoon stood in the doorway of the bar looking down the street toward the bank. "It's got to be secret service," Ralphy said. "They're the only ones that drive black SUV's like that. Probably bullet-proof, bomb-proof—probably has built in machine guns, too."

Witherspoon looked a Ralphy and laughed. "This isn't a James Bond movie. Could you tell who was in there? I wonder if the sheriff's with them? If he is, Marge will know everything that happens. I heard that when he comes, the commissioners are going to declare it Obama Day, make some kind of resolution or something so it will always be a holiday. I also heard they are going to hold some kind of ribbon cutting ceremony out at Thornberry's. I'm still trying to get a hold of Quince."

"Smitty said he saw his Cadillac yesterday at the bank," Ralphy said. "See, you don't use any common sense when it comes to this stuff. If I was looking for Quince, I'd go right to the source."

"And what's that?"

"Sally Butterbetter. Who do you think he's chasing when he's not making deals? A skirt. She probably has his personal cell number and knows where he's stayin' when he's in town. If nothing else, follow her. She probably goes to his motel when she gets off work. Jesse said she heard Sally was in his pocket big time."

Witherspoon thought about the revelation. "Last I heard she was making it with Roberts, her boss. She must really get around."

"I don't know, it just sounds smart to me. Go where the money is. She almost got it on with Edwards when he was here. That rumor wouldn't quit for a month."

They both retreated into the bar.

The SUV moved slowly down Main Street after making a complete recon of the outside of the bank. Next, they moved on to the hardware store, the only three-story building on the route toward the interchange. They stopped in front, and Carter took several pictures. Then they drove up the alley next to the store and took pictures of the rear.

As they pulled back out in front, turning onto Main Street, Wyeth, Stokes, and Carter were discussing the positioning of sharpshooters on the roof, and Miner saw Harold Hanover, owner of the hardware store, standing on the front walk holding a sign that proclaimed "WELCOME PRESIDENT OBAMA." Miner glanced at the other three, relieved that they hadn't noticed.

They continued out toward the interchange, passing the Hinkley Family Bowling Center. Stokes held his hand up without comment and Wyeth slammed on the brakes and pulled to the curb.

"You hit a cat or something?" Miner asked, bracing himself against the seat in front of him.

Stokes pointed toward the parking lot of the bowling center, and Carter took pictures. Next, Carter pulled a range finder from his camera bag and started taking point measurements of the parking lot.

Finally, Stokes said, "What do you think?"

"About what?" Miner said.

Wyeth looked into the rear view mirror and said, "He's not talking to you."

Miner crossed his arms again. "Oh, see, I don't understand big-time federal agent secret code talk like you guys. I'm just a small town sheriff that never went to federal agent school."

Carter ignored the commentary and said, "It's big enough. The power lines are on the other side of the road so they can land away from the building." Carter looked at Miner. "You know the owner?"

Miner stared out the window, ignoring the question.

Wyeth sighed and turned around in his seat. "Miner, he's asking you a question."

"Oh, you are talking to me?" Miner held up his hands, shrugging his shoulders. "I didn't know."

"Just answer the question, Miner, and quit the theatrics," Wyeth said, slumping down in the seat.

"Yeah, I know the owner. Toby Majewski. Why?"

The vehicle went silent again.

"Oh, another secret," Miner said, again looking out the window.

They approached the interchange, and Wyeth slowed to turn the vehicle around.

Miner said, "That's the Thornberry place where everyone thinks they're going to build an amusement park."

What do you mean 'thinks'?" Wyeth asked.

Miner laughed. "You don't think this is legit, do you? It's a con. I knew that from the start. Guy blows into town talking about building another Disneyland out in a cornfield, and everyone gets goggle-eyed. Oh, that means stupid. Might not be in the federal secret agent hand book."

"Not what the Treasury Department says," Wyeth said.

Stokes shook his hand at Wyeth to keep quiet.

"Oh, that's right. I'm not supposed to know what this is all about," Miner continued. "Well, I'll give you odds, ten to one, that after all of this hullabaloo blows over, there ain't gonna be any amusement park in that field. The only one that's gonna come out on top is ol' Thornberry sittin' up there on his porch. He got a big option on the ground, I heard, to make the deal sound real."

Carter said, "We really should talk to him. His barn and house are so close to the highway, we'll have to have someone positioned there if there is a motorcade."

Miner laughed again. "See that dog lying in the lane? If any of you can get down that driveway without shooting him, I'll buy you dinner tonight, but I won't pay your hospital bill."

Wyeth asked, "How do you get up to the house?"

"You don't. If Thornberry wants to talk to you, he'll come to the car; otherwise, you'll have to wait until he comes to town. He's not big on government messin' in his business, so with this car, and you guys lookin' like you're straight out of *Men in Black*, your chances are pretty slim." Miner looked back out the window, smiling.

"You know him pretty well?" Wyeth asked.

"Well enough."

Wyeth shook his head, frustrated with the banter, and said with attitude, "Well enough to get past the dog?"

"I suppose."

Stokes didn't say anything as he pointed for Wyeth to pull down the lane.

Wyeth drove up to Mack lying in the lane and stopped. "What do I do now?"

Miner responded, "I would suggest you not open your windows or doors until I talk to Thornberry."

"The dog won't go after you?" Carter asked.

Miner didn't respond as he opened his door and stepped out. Mack jumped up, baring his teeth, and slowly sneaked around the SUV. Miner just stood there, and when Mack showed his face around the front bumper he said, "Hey, Mack."

Mack stopped, wagged his tail, and went back and lay down in the lane.

Miner walked the distance to the porch, climbed the steps, and sat down on the swing next to Thornberry without addressing him. A moment passed, and he said, "Some government guys out there want to talk to you. Something about this amusement park deal you got goin'."

There was silence for a moment.

"Want a drink?" Thornberry asked. "Got some applejack in the cellar, make you holler at the moon."

"Don't mind if I do. Can you put an ice cube in it, tone it down a bit?"

Thornberry spit in the general direction of the end of the porch. "Shore, but it's better if you take it right outta the jug." He slowly got up and went inside, the screen door giving a stout bang behind him.

Miner heard Wyeth yelling out of the crack in his window as Mack gnawed at the door handle. "Miner, what's going on? Where did he go?"

Miner waved at them and smiled.

Thornberry returned with a jug and a dirty water glass with one ice cube in the bottom.

"I might need a lift back to town; looks like those boys are fixin' to leave me." Miner said with a smile.

"I wouldn't be too shore. Looks like Mack might have a holt of that front tire."

Ernest Eisley

CHAPTER 31

HINKLEY MESSENGER
October 6, 2009 Hinkley;
OH, MOMMA; IT'S OBAMA
Byline: Red Redderson, Editor

The stage is set for President Barrack Obama to arrive in Hinkley sometime between the hours of noon and one PM today. Security is said to be tight along the anticipated arrival route, although officials have been tight-lipped regarding the mode of transportation. A source within the State Police office in Cougar Falls indicates they have been placed on high alert in anticipation of a motorcade from the Cougar Falls airport to Hinkley via the interstate. Another official at O'Hare International in Chicago says a military transport helicopter is waiting to be used to shuttle the president direct to Hinkley from Air Force One. The official went on to say that the mode of transportation will not be announced until the last minute.

FIRST STATE BANK and (dis)TRUST of Hinkley County

The purpose of the president's visit, as described in a news release from the office of the president and distributed by the Associated Press, *is to congratulate and recognize the officials of the First State Bank and Trust of Hinkley County for their participation in the T.A.R.P. (Troubled Asset Relief Program) program. A source at the bank has confirmed that T.A.R.P. funds are instrumental in the financing of the recently announced hotel convention center project. The source further stated that the developer is scheduled to attend the reception. Jerome Roberts, CEO of First State Bank and Trust, was unavailable for comment, but his meeting with the president, along with other officials, has been confirmed.*

Advance security contingents have been active in the area for the past few days. Toby Majewski, owner of Hinkley Family Bowling Center stated that his parking lot is a main staging area for the arrival. He has offered a bowling special, good only for today—3 lines for $5, including popcorn and a drink to anyone that wants to witness the arrival of the president (see the ad and coupon on page 3).

Sheriff Miner indicated his department is playing a critical role in crowd and traffic control. "Our department is working hand-in-hand with the Secret Service to assure the safety of the president and all of the citizens of Hinkley County that come out to welcome him."

Sam Sadinski, recently appointed head of the Homeland Security and Emergency Management Department of Hinkley County said, "Our department will be supplying emergency medical assistance from our trailer and selling cold drinks just across the street from the bank. We are hoping the president will try our homemade lemonade."

The Main Street Business Association is holding a special Obama Week Stimulus Sidewalk Sale, with specials on all merchandise (see special color sale insert in today's paper).

Participants in the reception include the Hinkley High School Marching Band, which will be assembled near the Hinkley Bowling Center and will march to the First State Bank. The Hinkley County Horse and Bridle Synchronized Sidestepping

Stallions Club will follow the band and provide a synchronized riding demonstration immediately following the president's arrival and speech. The county commissioners will be present to award the president with a Hinkley County Golden Cow Bell, signifying agriculture as the primary industry of Hinkley County. Harold Hanover, owner of Hanover's Hardware and president of the local Chamber of Commerce, will have a special presentation, awarding the Small Business of the Year award to a yet-to-be-announced winner.

The president's agenda is expected to be limited to his initial remarks to the audience in the parking lot of the bank, a private meeting with the bank CEO, the developer, and officials from the Treasury Department, and a photo session with local officials. This is expected to last less than thirty minutes, according to a source at the sheriff's department.

By nine o'clock, sidewalks along Main Street were jammed with local residents and an equal number from surrounding communities, some sitting in lawn chairs with umbrellas and others leaning against store fronts or sitting on the curb. Vendors walked the street selling everything from balloons to tee shirts imprinted with "I got stimulated by President Obama" and others with a grinning, floppy eared cartoon face of the president." Food vendors lined the street selling elephant ears, corn dogs, and numerous other carnival delights.

Several local clubs and organizations had staked out special areas to display their banners and welcoming signs. The Hinkley County Underprivileged Rural Learning Services organization, locally known as HURLS, had a hand-painted banner spread between two lawn chairs displaying "WELCOME PRESIDENT OBAMMA." Once unraveled, the parents in charge realized the mistake, but felt compelled not to embarrass the class artists, so they took turns standing in front of the extra M as the crowds paraded by.

Ralphy opened an hour early to take advantage of the thirsty crowd, and his bar was full of patrons eager to take advantage of the Obama Special, a Bud Light with an Old Crow whiskey chaser for two bucks. Commissioner Ralph Bellows stood at the end of the bar dressed in his best suit, a napkin stuffed in his collar so he didn't spill any beer on his new polyester tie, explaining how he was going to review what economic impact the convention center/ amusement park would have on the county with the president during their private meeting. At the other end of the bar, patrons were placing bets on whether Bellows would still be able to walk when the anticipated visit took place.

Roger Witherspoon stood next to Bellows, still fishing for information. "Ralph, assuming this Quince guy really comes through, he's going to need somebody to manage his local affairs. Has he said anything about that? Who he might have in mind?"

Bellows took a shot of Old Crow in one gulp and followed it with a big draw on his beer mug. He then wiped his mouth with the sleeve of his suit coat and pushed the shot glass toward Ralphy with a wink.

"You know, Roger, this Quince is a pretty sly character. Now, I don't mean that in a bad way. I just mean he's pretty savvy when it comes to gettin' down to the nitty gritty, you know what I mean? Now, if I was to suggest to him that I knew a lawyer in town that would like to handle his local affairs, he'd step back and say to himself, 'Now what's this commissioner doin' trying to hump a local attorney? Must be some kind of hanky-panky goin' on.' You know what I mean? A guy in my position has to be careful. Can't be just recommending people. I'm a public official."

Roger made a fake choking sound as he drew on his beer. "That why your brother-in-law works in the engineer's office and your sister's daughter works in the court house? I suppose you didn't recommend them, either."

Bellows's end of the bar broke out in laughter. Bellows acted as if he didn't hear the comment and said, "Now, when we meet with Quince this afternoon, if he asks—and I'm not promising anything—but if he asks my opinion on a good local representative, I'll be happy to mention your name. Like I said—no promises." Bellows smiled and tossed down another shot.

The three major networks had studio trucks with satellite dishes parked on a side street next to the bank. CNN and Fox decided to forgo live transmission and had camera crews to tape the event. Oprah Winfrey had a personal studio truck on hand for a live interview since the event was scheduled during the taping of her show in Chicago. Her crew received special permission to set up an interview site inside the bank with appropriate lighting and background to do impromptu interviews with bank employees and hopefully with the president when he entered the bank for the private meeting.

The bank opened at nine o'clock and conducted normal business for one hour, and then promptly locked the doors. Secret Service agents entered the bank with bomb sniffing dogs and conducted a thorough search of the building, finally giving the all-clear and positioning three presumably heavily armed, dark-suited personnel in strategic positions on the balcony over the lobby and on the roof.

J.R. had arrived at the bank well in advance of any other employee and locked himself in his office.

Yusuf Olajuwon and Jasmine Jackson had spent the night at the Hinkley Motor Inn, and after a leisurely breakfast at Denny's, were en route to the bank in a loaner car provided by Fred Ribley from Fred's Fords, in exchange for a V.I.P. seat in the temporary bleachers assembled across the street from the entrance to the bank.

When Fred arrived, he found that there really wasn't any special V.I.P. seating and his hand-written invitation signed by Jasmine Jackson didn't mean squat to the Pasquali family, tomato farmers who had driven three hundred miles and sat on wooden bleachers since eight o'clock the night before.

After a lively discussion over the meaning of V.I.P. and a poorly chosen comment by Fred about Frank Pasquali's bib overalls, Fred retreated to Ralphy's and joined the other bar patrons for an Obama Special.

The bank schedule, as posted on the door and circulated to all employees, advised that after closing to the public at ten

FIRST STATE BANK and (dis)TRUST of Hinkley County

o'clock, there would be an hour to complete transactions, balance teller windows, and secure all securities and money. At eleven o'clock, all personnel except Secret Service would be asked to leave the building, and another sweep would be conducted. After the sweep, V.I.P.'s would be invited back in, searched with a metal detector, and then be allowed to loiter until the president arrived.

After balancing his bank and organizing his teller station, Pucker walked around the counter and stood in front of his station with his hands folded, waiting for further instruction.

The Oprah Winfrey temporary studio had been set up in the bank foyer with portable lighting, a cameraman with a hand-held camera, site director, and assistant, all talking on cell phones or fiddling with the equipment. The director said something to the assistant and she started roving around the bank lobby, finally walking up to Pucker.

"And what's your job at this bank?" the assistant asked.

Pucker hesitated and looked around, making sure he was the target of the question. "I'm a teller at this station, and I handle the drive-up window. I'm in the bank teller hall of fame," he finished with emphasis.

That was enough for the assistant. "Come with me." She grabbed Pucker's arm and pulled him toward the temporary studio.

Sally, sitting at her desk filing her nails, saw the abduction and walked over to the interview site as well, standing back to determine what was going on. She had assumed the camera and lighting was only for the president.

The assistant pushed Pucker from behind until they arrived in front of the site director, a very young looking man with unkempt hair matted by a headset, a t-shirt with an advertisement for a rock concert two years past, blue jeans with frayed holes in strategic places, and bloodshot eyes, evidence of a very late night.

"Who's this?" the director asked while he continued to listen to another conversation on his cell phone.

The assistant looked at Pucker, expecting him to answer, but received no reaction. "Uh, he's asking who you are. *Comprende?*"

Pucker stiffened. "My name is Ernest Eisley."

"Where'd you get that pen holder thing in your pocket?" the director asked, not expecting an answer. "I haven't seen one of those forever. Anyway, we are going to have you stand right over here. We are going to record this. You have to wear a headset because we are really screwed with this set up. The monitor isn't working, so you won't be able to see Oprah. You'll just have to listen to her questions in the headset and respond. Like I said, this isn't going to be live; it will be used as filler during the show, depending on the president's schedule."

Pucker asked, "This is going to be on television?"

The assistant looked at him with a cocked head and said with a load of sarcasm, as if she was talking to a two-year-old, "Duh, what do you think he is holding? It's a TV camera. It takes a picture of you and then it travels down this here long cord and magically appears in your living room; and that's how you get on TV."

The director said, "Okay, look, what's your name again?"

"Ernest, Ernest Eisley."

"Okay, Ernie. They're getting Oprah set up right now. When they are ready, we will turn the camera on here. See that thing right above the lens? Anyway, when the little red light comes on, that means the camera is on. As I said, we are taping, so this will be kind of casual. You will hear her in the headset, probably talking to the people in the audience in Chicago, getting them warmed up for the show, but eventually she will get to you and ask you some questions. Got it?"

"Questions about what?"

Sally, realizing what was going on, ran to J.R.'s office, and pounded on the door.

From inside she heard, "W-w-what?"

"You need to come out here. They are putting Pucker on the *Oprah Winfrey Show*."

"Oh, boy. Oh, boy, oh, boy, all the way. Don't let them do that; I'll be right there. Tell them to stay away."

Sally took a step back from the door, holding her hand over her mouth, trying to comprehend what she had just heard. *Was he singing?*

The assistant director straightened Pucker's shirt after fitting the small mike and earpiece on his head and made sure he was standing straight in front of the camera. "My, you have a nice set of pens and pencils there, Ernie. Okay, do you hear anything yet? It should be on, and you should be able to hear the floor in Chicago."

Pucker stared straight ahead and then nodded in acknowledgement.

J.R. busted through his office door, stopped next to Sally looking at the set across the lobby, and then marched with Sally in step right behind up to the director.

"W-w-w-what's going on? What's going on all the way? No one asked if you could do this. No one asked if this was okay."

The site director, the assistant, Sally, and everyone within earshot stared at J.R. with their mouths open, not knowing whether to laugh or run.

Then the director regained his composure and said, "Quiet, we are taping. It's just an interview; it's not live."

Sally looked at J.R. and said, "Interview with whom?"

The director looked at her with indignation and then, after taking in her appearance, said with less attitude, "It's with Oprah. She wants to put a personal touch on the show before talking to President Obama. Maybe we could get you on next. I think I could arrange that. What's your name?"

Sally looked at J.R., and then at Pucker, who seemed to have a pleading look on his face. She took J.R.'s arm and led him away. A few feet from the group, Sally said, "J.R., is something wrong? What's with the singing? No offense, but it's kind of strange."

J.R. didn't respond and just rubbed his forehead, shuffled back to his office, and slammed the door.

Sally walked back to the interview just in time to hear Pucker respond to an apparent question from Oprah.

In astonishingly clean cadence and exact punctuation, Pucker said, "Miss Winfrey, it is my pleasure to talk to you. Yes, I am an employee of the bank, a teller, in the bank teller hall of fame, by the way."

Sally could just barely hear the other side of the conversation through some of the earpieces, but she thought she heard the audience applauding. There was a few seconds of quiet, and then Pucker responded again.

"We are very proud to have been chosen by the president. This is a once-in-a-lifetime opportunity. I don't believe we have ever had a president visit Hinkley, and now that we have a colored president, it's just that much more important."

The assistant director looked at the director with eyes so wide Sally thought her face might explode. The director started to open his mouth and then screams erupted from all the earphones as Oprah responded. "What did you say? What did he say? Did he say what I think he said? I don't believe it. Did he say it?"

Pucker tried to adjust his headset to protect himself from a pierced eardrum.

Sally said to herself, "Oh, my god."

Pucker hesitated, apparently fielding another question. "Well, that's not what— I mean, I meant no disrespect. I just meant— No, that's not how we—I—refer to African-American people. I was just— Well, if that's how you feel— Yes, our bank is very friendly to those people. I mean— Yes, I understand. I didn't mean— Yes, ma'am. It's been very nice talking to you, as well. Thank you very much."

The assistant walked over to Pucker and yanked the headset off his head. "Nice job, Ernie. You may have just won an Emmy, or a spot on America's stupidest people." She turned to the director, who was listening on his cell phone. "You think she'll use it?"

FIRST STATE BANK and (dis)TRUST of Hinkley County

He waved his hand and then pulled the phone from his ear. "Man, is she pissed. I mean, to the max. They said she threw the water pitcher across the stage and hit some lady in the audience. That'll cost 'em a new car."

Sally walked over to Pucker and took him by the arm. "God, Pucker, I don't believe you said that." Then she laughed. "It was kind of funny. I don't think you have to worry about being on TV."

Monica Roberts

CHAPTER 32

At eleven o'clock, the bank was cleared and the final security check made. A checkpoint was set up at the front door, and those with security clearance were allowed back in. J.R. was the first through the metal detector. He went straight to his office and closed the door. Sally followed Monica Roberts, along with the entourage of commissioners, town officials, Olajuwon, Jasmine, and Sook Kim Chow.

Sheriff Miner casually walked through the door, and the agent checking the clearance list said, "I don't see your name on the list, sheriff. I thought you were supposed to monitor traffic."

Miner frowned and tried to look over the end of the clipboard the agent was holding, and said, "Must be a mistake. I'm the sheriff. If I want to be here, I'll be here."

The agent hesitated, turned his head to speak into his hidden microphone to get advice from a supervisor, and Miner walked around the portable metal detector. He walked up to

Sally sitting at her desk and sat on the corner, observing the impatient crowd milling around the lobby. "Where's J.R?"

"He's locked in his office. I'm not sure what's wrong."

"Where's the big developer guy? I thought he was supposed to be part of this."

Sally thought for minute and realized it was a good question. "I don't know. Maybe he'll show up when the president gets here."

Once all of the invited guests were back in the bank, the door was locked and guarded by a Secret Service agent.

Olajuwon and Chow walked up to Sally and the sheriff, who was now sitting in the chair next to her desk, and Olajuwon asked without acknowledging or looking at Miner, "Where's J.R?"

"Seems to be the question of the day," Sally responded. "He's in his office, and I don't think he wants to see anyone right now. He's not feeling very well."

"Got butterflies, huh?" Olajuwon smiled broadly. "What about Quince?"

Chow looked around Olajuwon with a concerned tone. "Yeah, where's Quince? He's supposed to be here." Chow's cell phone beeped loudly, and he flipped it open. "Yes, Mr. Secretary. Uh–huh. Everything is fine…… Well, the developer hasn't shown up yet, but— Yes, sir, I'll have them begin the search. Signing off, sir." Chow rushed over to the agent at the door and gave instructions, waving his arms and pointing in every direction. The agent spoke with the same emphasis into his hidden microphone.

Commissioner Bellows staggered up to Sally's desk, which was now nearly surrounded by anxious V.I.P.s. He put both hands on the desk to keep from tipping over and said, "Oh, hokay, here's whas we need to do. When Orama gess here, we all sing hate to the sheif. Hokay?"

Miner stepped over to Bellows and gently whispered in his ear.

Bellows got an alarmed look and shook his head. "Damn, hees already been here? Where wass I?" Bellows turned and tried to focus on the rest of the room. "Iss he still here?"

Miner bent down again and whispered.

"Hokay, iss there anything to eat down there?"

Miner took Bellows by the arm, holding him erect, and headed for the employee lounge. Miner turned as he walked away and said, "I'll be right back."

At eleven forty-five, the crowd around Sally's desk had dispersed as everyone anticipated the announcement that the president would soon arrive. Miner was still baby-sitting Bellows and besides a low undertone of casual conversation, the room was relatively quiet.

Sally saw another agent enter the front door and show identification to the guard. The new agent looked familiar, but his aviator sunglasses gave him the appearance of every other government security person milling around.

After talking for a few seconds to the door guard, the man started across the lobby, removing his glasses. "How you doin' today, darlin'?" Bit had his hair cut short and was wearing a dark suit with a white oxford shirt and striped tie—typical Secret Service attire. His cowboy boots were gone and the only remaining recognizable fixture was his big smile.

Sally leaned so far forward on her desk staring at Bit as he approached that she almost fell out of her chair. "Bit? I don't believe it. You look so, so normal."

Bit took a step back and did a way too-obvious self-examination, smiled at Sally, and said, "Like it? It's the new me."

"Can't say that I do, but then, can't say that I don't. You look like every other government guy walking around here talking into their coat."

"Yeah, there's a lot of that. Where's J.R.?"

Sally frowned. "He's locked in his office. Hasn't come out all morning except when we had to leave the building. Then he ran back in there and we haven't seen him since."

"Well it's time for him to come to the show. Why don't you call him and tell him I'm here. Then go get Olajuwon and his friends, and we'll have a little get together in his office. You know, if we get this done right quick, we'll have time to get some

FIRST STATE BANK and (dis)TRUST of Hinkley County

of that Texas red chili and a cold beer." Bit winked at her and went back to talk to the guard at the door.

Sally called J.R. He picked up the phone, but didn't say anything. Sally hesitated. She heard J.R. breathing into the phone and said, "God, J.R., you better suck it up, buddy. Anyway, Bit is here, and he wants to meet with you and the big black guy and his friends in your office. I'm sending them in." As she hung up, she heard J.R. stuttering something unintelligible.

She rounded up Olajuwon, Jasmine, and Chow and ushered them to the office door. As they approached, Monica was pounding on the door and yelling to be let in. J.R. opened the door a crack to tell her to go away, and she pushed the door open, cracking him in the nose.

J.R. stumbled backwards, and the whole group piled into the office. J.R. backed up, and holding his nose, hurriedly moved around his desk to place some distance between him and the group.

Monica immediately leaned on the desk and said, "What in heaven's name is going on, J.R.? You don't talk to me, you don't call me." She turned and pointed a long finger at Sally standing near the door. "It's her, isn't it? It's that little tramp you call an assistant, isn't it?"

Sally opened her mouth to defend herself, but Monica continued. "Let me give you some news, sister. You don't work here anymore, got it?" She turned to J.R. and said, "What do you think about that, Mr. Roberts? Or maybe you would rather screw her and lose half of this bank along with half of everything else you own. Huh? I don't hear anything, J.R. The cat got your tongue?"

J.R. looked like he had a mouth full of cotton. His cheeks were puffed out and his face was red. He opened his mouth, but nothing came out, then he closed his eyes and concentrated. "I don't know. I don't know what you are talking about all the way. This is a bad time. Let's do this another day."

J.R.'s rhythmic cure momentarily halted Monica's confrontation, and she stared at him along with the rest of the group, eyes wide with astonishment. But Monica sensed a rat in the closet. She looked at J.R. with a scowl and said through clenched teeth, "Are you making fun of me? Do you think this is funny? I'll show you what funny is, you slime bag womanizer." She looked at J.R.'s desk and after some contemplation, picked up one of his prized possessions, a glass enclosed pedestal holding a baseball signed by Babe Ruth and several other influential baseball players. Removing the ball she prepared to pitch it through the window behind the desk.

Bit stepped into the room behind Sally, saw Monica doing her wind up, and said, "Whoa, there. Hold that curve ball, honey. We don't want anyone to get hurt here."

Sally said, "Mrs. Roberts, I don't know where you are getting your information, but Bit and I here have been going together for quite a while, isn't that right, Bit? I don't know how I could have time to do whatever you think I was doing with your husband when I spend most of my nights with Bit. Isn't that right, Bit?"

All of the eyes in the room were on Bit. He had lost his big smile but didn't respond.

Monica said, "Who the hell is Bit?" and started her wind up again.

Bit raised his hands and said, "Sorry I interrupted this little domestic squabble, but there just ain't time to deal with it right now." He walked over to Monica, and with some difficulty, removed the baseball from her hand. "Now, Mrs. Roberts, if you'll excuse us, we have some business to tend to. Why don't you go outside, and Sally can do some more explaining." He looked sternly at Sally and said, "Ain't that right, Miss Sally?"

Sally did a quick turn on her tiptoes and exited. Monica stood her ground for a brief minute, but when Bit gave her the same stern look and tilted his head toward the door she relented— not without looking at J.R. and saying, "Slime bag."

As Monica stepped through the door, Murt Featherstone peeked in. "You ready for us? Henry's out here, too. Henry," she yelled and looked back in. "He's kinda hard a hearin'." She looked back out and yelled again. "Henry, get in here."

FIRST STATE BANK and (dis)TRUST of Hinkley County

The shock of the argument was wearing off, and Chow decided to take charge. "What are th-these people doing here?"

Chow, dressed in his finest business suit acted like being close to Henry Thornberry, dressed in his reasonably clean dungarees, might pollute his personal space. After taking a step away from from the old man, he attempted to assert his authority. "We have to get organized. Quince, it doesn't help that you show up an hour late. The president will be here," he looked at his watch, "well, any minute now, I guess. Okay, here is the way I have it choreographed."

"Whoa, slow down there, slick; we got a few things to discuss first." Bit moved around the desk and sat on the corner, resting his hand on the carved lion's head.

Olajuwon said, "We will have plenty of time to put together all of the details after the event is over. Right now, we just need to know who is going to give the general description of the project to the president."

"Well, unfortunately," Bit said in a more serious tone, "there's not going to be any meeting with the president. See, Rickie, the party's over. I want you all to meet Rickie Harris, a.k.a. Rickie the Rocket, a.k.a. Rick Harrison, a.k.a. Yusuf Hussein Olajuwon. Rickie here has been working a scam—"

Olajuwon interrupted abruptly. "What? Who do you think you are talking to? You're nothing but an Okie acting like a big-time investor, and you are trying to run stories on me?" Olajuwon pulled out a leather flip fold and displayed it by holding it up over his head. "This credential is authentic, signed by the Secretary of the Treasury, and it gives me—"

Sheriff Miner opened the door with flare and walked in. "You all ready for the big show? All those guys out there are talking into their coats, so he must be getting close. Now, I think it's important that I be included in any interview with the President. It's important to show the involvement of our local law enforcement." Miner straightened his tie and adjusted his shirt collar as he talked.

Everyone turned to look at Miner and then back at Olajuwon.

"Sheriff, arrest this man," Olajuwon said pointing at Quince and holding up his picture I.D. from the Treasury Department so Miner could get a look. "He's a fraud, and I have evidence that he is involved in a scheme to defraud this bank out of millions of dollars. I was withholding this information until after this event, hoping not to embarrass our department and the president, but it can't be helped."

Chow's knees started to buckle and he said, "What are we doing? You can't do this now; the president will be here any minute."

Miner got a big smile on his face. "I knew it. I knew it right from the start. Didn't I tell you, J.R.? Nobody would listen to ol' Reg. No, nobody wanted to believe me. Well, son, it'll be a pleasure puttin' the collar on this hound dog." Miner hesitated for a second and then with a broad smile said, "Why don't we wait and we can do this in front of the cameras, kind of like *America's Most Wanted*?"

Chow pulled out his cell phone, hit the speed dial, and turned toward the door yelling into the phone "Mr. Secretary, abort, abort, we have a problem." As he briskly walked out, they heard him say, "It's bigger than Apollo Thirteen. Abort, abort."

Miner, still smiling broadly, walked over to Bit. "Where's that big puppy dog smile now, blue eyes?"

Bit gave Murt a wink, she looked at Thornberry, and they both grinned.

"Hold on there, sheriff, let me look here." Bit reached inside his jacket and pulled out his own flip fold. "Hot damn, looky there. It's a get out of jail free card."

Miner bent down to examine the badge and photo I.D. Bit continued, "See that fine print right there on the badge?" He pointed as if he was instructing a three-year-old. "A.T.F. You know what that is, don't you, Sheriff? See this little thing here? Special Service. That means I can be one mean son of a bitch if I want to."

Miner continued to examine the I.D. "It says your name is Robert Quince. I thought everyone said your name was Bite or Bit or something."

"Actually, Bitter was my daddy's name. Made a pretty good cover once they changed his birth date and such."

Olajuwon bellowed in his old man river voice, "This is bullshit. He's a fraud. Get him out of here before the president gets here."

Sally stuck her head in the door and reported, "The helicopter just flew by; they say he'll be here shortly." She closed the door.

Murt looked at Thornberry and said, "Damn, this is gettin' fun."

Henry responded, "They got anything to drink around here?"

Olajuwon stepped forward, trying to use his size to influence the impending decision. "This is getting out of hand, sheriff; get him out of here. The President will be here any minute. Get him out of here and we will conduct the meeting without him."

Bit smiled, looking at his flip fold, and said, "Wait a minute. Looky here. Here's a card that says I can kick your ass if I want, and if I look a little deeper, there's probably one in here that says I can shoot your ass, too." With a stern voice he continued, "So back off, Rickie."

Sally stuck her head back in the door. "Somebody said the helicopter kept going and didn't land, and all of the black-suited guys are disappearing. It's like they called the whole deal off." Sally slid inside before closing the door. She moved next to Murt and whispered, "What's goin' on in here?"

"This is more fun than a pocket full o' mice in church." Murt looked over Sally's shoulder and said, "Hold on a minute."

Jasmine was moving toward the door, back stepping slowly, and nonchalantly looking around the room, hoping no one noticed.

Murt moved next to her as she reached for the door handle. "Goin' somewheres? Why don't you stick around and see what happens? I ain't suggestin'; I'm tellin'. Get your skinny ass back over there."

Jasmine thought of holding her ground, but noticed everyone in the room was looking at her, and walked over and bounced down in the big chair.

Miner decided to take charge. "Okay, Quince, you seem to have the ace in the hole. What's going on here?"

Olajuwon started to interrupt, but Miner beat him to the punch. "You keep your mouth shut. You'll get your turn, maybe."

Bit thought for a few seconds. "Okay, you want to know? I'll give you the short story. Ol' Rickie the Rocket here, he got his name by playin' runnin' back for 'Ol Miss'; he wormed his way into the Treasury Department, appointed by a brother in Washington that was appointed by the new administration. He's no dummy. Came out of St. Louis where he landed after gettin' booted from school for runnin' a telephone scam selling stolen tests. Pretty well educated, but really hadn't hit the big time until he talked his way into this appointment. I'm not sure how that came about, but when we start talking wire fraud, interstate bank fraud, conspiracy, and a few other felonies, I think we'll find out who worked him into the system.

"Anyway, Rickie anointed himself a Muslim and changed his name, set up a new consulting company, and started strong-arming small banks with fraudulent projects. Once the bank comes on board, he installs his consulting company, and they walk away with a big percent of the take. Most of the time, the project fails. There have been three before this one. I've been on Rickie's tail for the last six months, and Hinkley just happened to work out perfect for a little personal parley with Mr. Harris. Murt and Henry agreed to play along, and J.R.—" Bit turned and looked at J.R. "He smelled a rat, so I tuned him in as well."

J.R., standing behind the desk, said, "I-I-I-I knew it was. I knew it was. I knew it was all the way. Nobody's gonna con me—nobody named Hussein, anyway."

Miner looked at J.R. and said, "J.R., you may have had too much caffeine this morning." Turning, he looked at Olajuwon, "Rickie or Olajuwon, or whatever—what have you got to say for yourself? It better be good because the current don't seem to be runnin' in your favor."

Murt looked at Thornberry and said, "This oughta be good."

Thornberry headed for the door. "I need a drink."

Jasmine leaned forward, put her face in her hands, peeking through her fingers, and said, "I didn't know anything about this."

Olajuwon's eyes bulged, and he bellowed, "I'm an official of the United States Treasury Department, and no tin-horned sheriff or Okie cowboy is gonna—"

Everyone turned to see Thornberry's back as he exited and Chow step in with his cell phone at his ear. "Yes, sir. Yes, sir. I understand, sir."

Olajuwon said, "Miss Jackson, let's go. I've heard enough. Sheriff, you have made a big mistake. When this is over, you won't have a badge and you'll be looking for a new job." He pulled Jasmine up by the arm and turned for the door. Murt stood guard and looked at Bit, who winked and shook his head, advising her to give ground.

Miner started to reach for Olajuwon. Bit held up his hand and said quietly, "Don't bother; they won't get out the front door. I've two men outside with the arrest warrants waiting for us to come out."

As the door swung shut, they heard Olajuwon bellowing as the agents grasp his arms and he was read his rights.

Chow continued to apologize into his phone. "Yes, sir, Mister Secretary, but there was no way for me to know— I understand. Okay, that sounds good. I mean, you have made a good decision....... I understand. It was the president's decision, and it was a good one........ No, I realize what I think doesn't matter......... Yes, sir, signing off, sir." Chow plopped down in the big chair and muttered, "Five years of kissing ass down the tubes."

Bit said, "How'd it go out there? You get a chance to talk to Oprah?"

Chow leaned forward with a strained look on his face. "You couldn't wait another fifteen minutes, huh? You couldn't wait long enough to let the president give his remarks, let these people have their fifteen minutes of fame. But oh, no, you have to make a big deal out of this misunderstanding."

Bit smiled. "Ain't no misunderstanding, just facts. I have a file that would choke a buffalo, two of 'em, as matter of fact—recorded conversations, conspiratorial solicitations—you name it, I've got it. Ol Rickie is goin' away for quite a while. You want to join him?"

Chow's mouth dropped open as his face reddened. "I had no part in this. I did nothing wrong."

"Then I would suggest you quit whining and skedaddle out of here."

Chow glanced around him, jumped up, and hurried for the door.

Murt walked over and sat down, replacing Chow. "Damn, that was fun. You get to do this all the time?"

"It ain't always this much fun," answered Bit. "But sometimes I get to shoot 'em, so that makes up for it."

They all laughed, except for J.R., who tried, but could only hum.

CHAPTER 33

ASSOCIATED PRESS
Wednesday October 7, 2009
Hinkley, Illinois:
OBAMA CANCELS TOWN MEETING

President Obama abruptly cancelled a town meeting in Hinkley, Illinois, that had only been announced two days before. The original White House press release said the meeting was to honor local business representatives and bank officials for their efforts in utilizing T.A.R.P. funds to stimulate the local economy.

Immediately following the cancellation, the White House press secretary released a statement indicating the president had to interrupt his travel plans due to a national security issue. The press secretary did not elaborate on the exact nature of the security issue, although the president continued on his trip to Los Angeles to meet with Governor Schwarzenegger and House Majority Leader Nancy Pelosi to discuss the twenty-billion-dollar loan to financially strapped California.

FIRST STATE BANK and (dis)TRUST of Hinkley County

Residents of Hinkley County seemed dismayed by what the local Chamber of Commerce President Harold Hanover called a snub by the president. "He flew right over and kept going. It was as if he looked down and decided we weren't worth the effort. The people of this community really came out and showed their appreciation, and what good did it do?"

The local sheriff's office responded to inquiry with a written statement saying they had uncovered a conspiracy that, while not threatening to the president, was serious enough to cancel the event. The president's press secretary said his office was not aware of such allegations.

The president was scheduled to appear live on the **Oprah Winfrey Show** *from the Hinkley meeting site. Winfrey's correspondent indicated that although disappointed, Miss Winfrey felt it was probably best given the unruly nature of the audience, an assessment based on her camera crew's report.*

The president's travel plans include a stop in Houston following his meeting in Los Angeles and then a return to Washington. There has been no announcement indicating the Hinkley town meeting will be rescheduled.

HINKLEY MESSENGER
October 10, 2009
OBAMA A NADA
Hinkley, Illinois;

President Obama did a fly-by Tuesday, and apparently did not like what he saw. The president's press secretary said, "There were circumstances beyond the president's control that prevented the short visit in Hinkley County. The president is truly sorry and applauds local officials for their efforts to create jobs and affect the national economic turn around." In a written statement released by the press secretary, a matter of national security was cited as the reason for the abrupt cancellation of the visit.

The president was scheduled to arrive by helicopter at 12:07 PM and land at the Hinkley Family Bowling Center on Main Street. A motorcade would have then transported the president and his entourage to the First State Bank and Trust for a brief speech, followed by a private meeting with county officials and bank management. The crowd up and down Main Street and assembled near the bank was estimated at twenty thousand. At approximately 12:15 PM, two military helicopters passed overhead and then left the area. Within minutes, all security personnel, with the exception of local authorities, vacated as well. By 1:00, all of the network television personnel and equipment disappeared.

Sheriff Miner reported that although the crowd became unruly after Harold Hanover, president of the local Chamber of Commerce announced the cancellation of the event, the only arrest resulted from an altercation outside of Ralphy's restaurant on Main Street when a patron leaving the restaurant tripped over a lawn chair and began arguing with the owner. Sheriff Deputies arrested William Bupkiss for disorderly conduct and public intoxication.

The White House press secretary gave no indication that the president's visit would be re-scheduled.

HINKLEY MESSENGER
October 10, 2009
HOTEL/CONVENTION CENTER PROJECT FIZZLES
Hinkley, Illinois;

A statement released by the Chamber of Commerce late Friday stated that the planned hotel/convention center project scheduled to break ground early next year has been delayed indefinitely. The statement went on to say that circumstances surrounding the financing were the cause of the delay.

Calls to the Hinkley County commissioners' office were not returned, although an anonymous source within the courthouse stated, "The developer has apparently disappeared after being exposed by the bank as not having the means originally declared. In addition, other suspicious circumstances were revealed by the government agency backing the financing."

John White, vice president and current manager in charge of operations at the First State Bank and Trust of Hinkley County said in a statement to the press, "After lengthy investigation,

FIRST STATE BANK and (dis)TRUST of Hinkley County

it was determined by the bank's commercial lending department that the proposed financing was not in the best interest of the bank. We do not know if the developer will seek alternative financing."

It was earlier learned that Henry Thornberry had agreed to sell a portion of his farm near the interstate highway interchange to accommodate the development. Mr. Thornberry refused to comment regarding the disposition of the contract of sale.

The developer's local representative, Roger Witherspoon of Witherspoon and Witherspoon stated, "I cannot comment on the current status of the project other than to say it has been delayed due to circumstances the developer prefers not to discuss. There have been allegations of misconduct that could lead to civil litigation, but there have been no actions filed at this time."

Unconfirmed reports have circulated that the dissolution of the hotel/convention center project was the reason President Obama cancelled his visit to the Hinkley community. Attempts to contact the developer have been unsuccessful.

❖

HINKLEY MESSENGER
Business Section
October 10, 2009
BANK MANAGEMENT SHAKEUP
Hinkley, Illinois;

A news release issued by the First State Bank and Trust Company of Hinkley County states that Jerome Roberts, great-grandson of one of the bank's founding members, current C.E.O. and president, will be replaced by John White, former chief financial officer. White will assume the position of executive vice president and chief managing officer of the bank. Roberts will remain president and assume the position of chairman of the board of directors. Although the news release did not give a reason for the change, a source within the bank stated that Jerome Roberts suffers from a medical condition that may limit his ability to manage the bank's affairs on a daily basis.

The press release went on to state Jerome Roberts's career at the bank spans over twenty-five years, and his leadership is credited with the bank being named as one of the top five most profitable banks in the state for the past three years.

John White joined the bank in 2001 as a bank teller and assumed the roll of auditor after completing his undergraduate degree in business finance from the University of Phoenix. He was appointed chief financial officer by the board of directors in 2008.

Bit, Sally, and Murt sat on Henry Thornberry's front porch while Mack lay in the driveway, protecting the premises. Henry brought out some lemonade that smelled a little like turpentine to Sally, so she passed when offered a glass.

Thornberry said, "I guess I missed the best part."

"I thought I was gonna bust when that big feller told the sheriff to arrest you," Murt said to Bit. "And then you tell him if he don't shut up you might shoot him. I swear, I think he almost turned white."

Bit said, "Now, Murt, honey, I don't remember threatening to shoot anybody. You may have wanted me to, just to liven things up, but I didn't even have a gun. That kinda stuff scares me."

"Damn, sorry I missed that," Thornberry said, taking a big swig out of the pitcher of lemonade he was holding on his lap.

Sheriff Miner pulled down the lane in his big patrol SUV and stopped just short of Mack. He rolled down his window and said, "Okay, Mack, move it over."

Mack slowly stood, raised his snout in the air and sniffed, turned, and walked toward the porch at a leisurely pace.

Miner made his way to the porch and exchanged greetings as he leaned against the sagging railing. He said to Bit, "You back in town to stay?"

"Little harder to follow when I'm drivin' a rental, huh?"

"Not followin'," Miner responded. "Just interested when a fed comes to town. You never know what they are gonna uncover, or claim to, anyway." Miner smiled.

FIRST STATE BANK and (dis)TRUST of Hinkley County

"I just had a few loose ends to take care of—the one hangin' on the end of this swing most of all."

Sally's smile was so big it made her face contort.

Thornberry said, "Little taste, sheriff? I can get ya a glass and some ice—or you can just dive into this here pitcher."

Murt looked at her Bugs Bunny watch and noted the ears meant it was time to go back to work. She grunted as she got up, walked over to Bit, and gave him a hug. "Shore wish you had taken me up on that farm inspection."

Bit winked at Sally. "I never said no to that offer. Just takin' my time answerin'."

Thornberry smiled. "She wantin' to take you to the barn? What about me, Murt?"

Murt smiled back. "You old fart, who'd want to roll in the hay with you? It'd take a week to heal up from the whisker burn."

Murt walked off the porch and headed for her car.

Miner started again. "No, I just wanted to know how all the trouble at the bank worked out."

"Well, a few heads rolled. Chow wasn't involved, but that didn't help him none. Far as I know, he's probably typing memos somewhere in North Dakota. You can't get fired from the government.

"Since this came from the inside and there's bad blood between the FBI and the treasury, the S.B.A. people, they're the one's that were getting burned the worse, assigned it to ATF, and we set up the sting. Geithner didn't even know, and man, was he pissed. He and Emanuel both are trying to get my boss and me fired. As I said—can't get fired from the government, so I'm not worried.

"Rickie the Rocket is out on bond; it'll be a year or two before anything happens, and I suspect he'll be history by then. Either he'll disappear on his own or someone will make him disappear. And I'm back to runnin' down leads on cigarette smugglers and illegal guns."

"Not much of that around here," Miner said sarcastically.

"Yeah, I know; that's why my expense account will show I had to visit you. You don't mind, do you, sheriff?"

"Naw. I mean, I wouldn't ever do that, but as you said, they can't fire you. Henry, maybe I will have a touch of that lemonade."

Epilogue

The file on the president's desk was no less than one hundred pages, with little colored flags extending from the cover, highlighting sections with names like Olajuwon, Chow, and Jackson. There was even a section for Quince. The room was silent. Geithner sat on the edge of the couch, pencil in hand, impatiently tapping it on a note pad. Vice President Biden leaned against a wall next to the couch, examining an imperfection in the wallpaper surrounding the fireplace mantel. Seated next to Geithner was Kent Sampson, special agent for the F.B.I., assigned to the investigation of the great Hinkley County fiasco.

The president leafed through the report, occasionally stopping at a page and examining the contents. "What about this Chow? What happened to him?"

Sampson cleared his throat. "Well, he was suspended with pay for thirty days and then reassigned to an I.R.S. office in Cincinnati, running collections."

Biden laughed aloud, shook his head, and said, "The guy embarrasses the president on national T.V. and gets a thirty-day vacation. That the best the F.B.I. can do? You know, when I was chairman of the—"

Sampson interrupted and directed his response to the president. "Sir, we could only try to clean up this mess. If we had been brought in ahead of time, maybe—"

Geithner threw up his hand and interrupted, "How could that happen when your department won't talk to the Secret Service or the A.T.F.?" He turned to the president, who was still evaluating the report. "Everything looked good to my people. We obviously had a breach of security when this Harris character got into such a, a position of authority, but that's not my department's responsibility." Geithner wiggled his index finger in the air to emphasize his point. "The F.B.I. does the due diligence on political appointments."

FIRST STATE BANK and (dis)TRUST of Hinkley County

The president held up his hand motioning for quiet, still looking at the report, and then laid it down on his desk and rubbed his face with his other hand, his expression not revealing his feelings. "Look, my grandmother had an expression she used in cases like this—and believe me, my grandmother was not known for vulgarity—but she would say, 'Excuses are like assholes. Everyone's got one, and they all stink.' Gentlemen, I am tired of excuses. Oprah called me last week; I only wish I had her on staff to straighten things out. If you had heard her description of how screwed up this was, you would both be thinking about sending out resumes." He picked up the report and threw it in the trash bucket behind his desk. "History. It's history. Look, everyone's thinking about healthcare now, so let's hope it doesn't get screwed up too."

Witherspoon sipped his beer, staring at the sweat-beaded glass as if it was his last in this lifetime. He was the only mid-afternoon patron in the bar and had been sitting in the same spot since before the lunch crowd arrived. Now he had witnessed their departure.

Ralphy walked out of the back room, having completed the after-lunch cleanup and prep for the dinner patrons. "You still mumbling into your beer? What's your problem today?"

"It's this town. Live here, die here, and what does it get you? Nothing."

"You still pining over that amusement park deal? It was all a scam. I knew it right from the start. Guy comes in here flashin' money—you could see it comin' a mile away."

Witherspoon looked up without expression. "Seems to me you are about the only one that made out on the deal. Had the biggest day you've had in years, didn't you say?"

"That's got nothing to do with it bein' a scam. If that's what it takes to get people out and into the bar, I'm all for it." Ralphy threw a towel over his shoulder and leaned on the bar. "You remember that first day—What was his name? Quince, that's it—the first time he walked in here, I said to you, that guy's a con artist if I ever saw one."

Witherspoon shook his head and gave an antagonistic laugh, still staring at his beer.

"What?" Ralphy asked defensively.

"He was the law. He was F.B.I. or something. Murt told me that. She wasn't sure, or at least she wouldn't say who called him in, but apparently, there was some kind of hanky-panky goin' on at the bank. That's why Roberts got canned. Con man, right. That's why you've been busted twice for serving minors. You couldn't tell a cop from a con man to save your life."

The front door opened, and with a whoosh of fall air, Ralph Bellows stepped in, rubbing his hands together and scurrying to the bar, absorbing the stool next to Witherspoon with his rotund posterior.

Without request, Ralphy poured Bellows a double whiskey with a short beer chaser. Bellows downed the shot with one gulp, followed it with a sip of beer, and then rubbed his chin with the back of his hand.

"Damn, it's cold out there," he said, looking at Witherspoon. "You look like you just lost your best friend. Oh, wait. You're an attorney. You don't have any friends." Bellows burst out in a hearty laugh and shoved the shot glass down the bar toward Ralphy.

"I may be near the bottom rung of the ladder," Witherspoon responded, "but when they step off, it's on some politician's face."

The ridicule didn't even faze Bellows as he waited in eager anticipation for his refill.

Ralphy came back and refilled the shot glass. "Didn't you have a commissioners' meeting today? First Tuesday of the month?" Ralphy asked.

Bellows took his time examining the amber liquid in the shot glass and then, as if an alarm sounded commencing a drinking contest, he gulped the double down in one swallow. He belched, slid his hand across his chin one more time, and shivered a little, the bite of the whiskey finally hitting home in the pit of his stomach. "Quick meeting. Not much on the agenda this month. Did get a letter from the president."

FIRST STATE BANK and (dis)TRUST of Hinkley County

The revelation was so nonchalant that it didn't register with Ralphy or Witherspoon for a few seconds, and then they both looked at each other.

Ralphy took the lead. "You talking about Obama?"

Bellows had his eyes closed, his hands resting on his stomach, almost as if he was coaxing the alcohol into his bloodstream. He responded without opening his eyes. "He's still the president, isn't he?"

Witherspoon sighed and shook his head, looking at Ralphy, and then with lack of expression said, "Okay, Ralph, so what did the president have to say?"

Bellows opened one eye and stared at the empty shot glass, and then slowly the bloodshot eye focused on Ralphy before closing again, the insinuation that a refill was required to get more information not lost on the bartender.

"Soon as we hear about the letter," Ralphy said, his arms crossed.

"Well," Bellows began, leaning forward and putting his elbows on the bar with his hands folded in front. "He wanted to apologize for the way the whole visitation thing went bust. Not exactly his words, but you know what I mean. Blamed it on some national security issue that came up. Anyway, he kind of left the door open. I mean, the way he said it he might re-schedule some day. Also invited any of us—any of us that cast our votes in the D column—that ever get to Washington to call his office, and we can get free passes to visit the White House. Thought that was nice of him. That's about it." Bellows reached his hand out and slowly pushed the shot glass toward Ralphy.

While Ralphy poured another double, Witherspoon leaned back, hooking his thumbs through his suspenders, and said, "Whole town gets a hard on, makes up signs—hell, it probably cost twenty thousand dollars in overtime for the security and cleanup—and for what? He decides at the last minute he's got something better to do."

"Can't trust people like that," Ralphy chimed in. "And did you hear what Opie said?"

"Who?" Witherspoon asked, looking up from his now-empty glass.

"Opie, the broad with all the money and the T.V. show."

Witherspoon shook his head and gave a slight laugh. "Oprah. Oprah Winfrey."

"Yeah, whatever. Anyway, my wife said she made some comment on her show about Hinkley—that we are still living in the dark ages, a bunch of racists. She even hinted that the Klan might still be active down here."

Bellows lifted himself from the bar stool, listed a little to port, corrected, straightened his jacket, and said, "Iss people like her that gif us a bad name."

One year later.

Monica Roberts leaned over and whispered to J.R. "Aren't the flowers beautiful? Jason must have been collecting funeral flowers all week to decorate the church like this." She held her hand over her mouth and laughed. J.R. stared straight ahead, stoic and unresponsive, thinking to the tune of an old Jimmy Hendrix song *I have to find a way out of here.*

Margaret Butterbetter, standing on the first step of the altar, finished the last note of *Ave' Maria,* and as tear laden eyes were dabbed and noses were blown, she made her way to the first aisle of the bride's side of the church, which was filled nearly to capacity. The groom's side was sparsely populated, most sitting to the rear as spill over from the other side.

There was looming silence as everyone anticipated the organ prelude for *Here Comes the Bride.* It was the practice of Pastor Butterbetter to give a prayer before the service began, recognizing God's work in bringing the two families together, having God speak through him, reminding the congregation that the church's work was only possible through generous tithes by members and offerings from guests. Although no formal offering would be taken during the service, offertory plates would be strategically positioned at each exit.

Pastor Butterbetter ended with a booming amen, retreated to the back of the altar, and stood awaiting the procession.

FIRST STATE BANK and (dis)TRUST of Hinkley County

Mary Transki started the processional prelude with an organ riff from Beethoven's *Eighteen-Twelve Overture*, something she had practiced ever since taking up playing the organ, and on the final slide down the note-laden keyboard, she finally broke into the recognizable *Here Comes the Bride.*

Sally Butterbetter, veiled in sanctimonious virgin white, baby's breath and tiny daisies intertwined in her hair, a bouquet of red roses firmly grasped and held against her chest, started the methodical march down the middle aisle of the Body of Christ on the Cross Baptist Church. Cameras flashed and babies cried as she took her steps, finally reaching the first step of the altar.

Pastor Butterbetter stepped up to Sally and began the ceremony. "As father of the beautiful creature standing before me and God the Father, I release her into the wondrous covenant of marriage and invite her to step forward with her new partner to begin the voyage that has guided civilization on God's path to eternal life. Friends, gather with me as we, a community of God and followers of Jesus Christ's teachings, send this couple on life's glorious journey. Step forward to recite the covenants that will govern the rest of your lives.

"Sally, do you take this man to be your lawfully wedded husband—to honor, to cherish, and to comfort until death do you part? If you agree, say I do."

As a tear lazily traversed her cheek, Sally answered, "I do."

"Ernest, do you take this woman…"

The end

www.ingramcontent.com/pod-product-compliance
Lightning Source LLC
Chambersburg PA
CBHW031639040426
42453CB00006B/153